Waterfowl

OF EASTERN NORTH AMERICA

Waterfowl

OF EASTERN NORTH AMERICA

Chris G. Earley

FIREFLY BOOKS

A FIREFLY BOOK

Published by Firefly Books Ltd. 2005

First Printing

Publisher Cataloging-in-Publication Data (U.S)

Earley, Chris G.
    Waterfowl of Eastern North America /
    Chris G. Earley. –1st ed.
[160] p. : col. photos. ; cm.
Includes bibliographical references and index.
Summary: A field guide to ducks, swans, geese and other duck-like birds. Includes detailed descriptions of markings, flight characteristics, migration, plumage changes and detailed comparison charts.
ISBN 1-55407-058-9
ISBN 1-55407-057-0 (pbk.)

1. Waterfowl — North America.
2. Waterfowl — Identification — North
    America. I. Title.

598. 41 22   QL696.A5E37   2005

Library and Archives Canada Cataloguing in Publication

Earley, Chris G., 1968-

Waterfowl of eastern North America /
Chris G. Earley.

Includes bibliographical references and index.
ISBN 1-55407-058-9 (bound).
ISBN 1-55407-057-0 (pbk.)

1. Waterfowl—East (U.S.)—Identification.
2. Waterfowl—Canada, Eastern—
    Identification. I. Title.

QL696.A52E27 2005 598.4'1'0974
C2004-906069-4

Published in the U.S. by
Firefly Books (U.S.) Inc.
P.O. Box 1338, Ellicott Station
Buffalo, New York 14205

Published in Canada by
Firefly Books Ltd.
66 Leek Crescent
Richmond Hill, Ontario L4B 1K1

Cover photos by Robert McCaw
Design by Lind Design
Printed and bound in China

The Publisher acknowledges the financial support of the Government of Canada through the Book Publishing Industry Development Program for its publishing activities.

Table of Contents

Wonderful waterfowl

SOME OF THE FIRST MEMORIES that many of us have of birds are feeding ducks in the local park or seeing a flock of geese flying in a "V" overhead. As beginning birders, we may have received a confidence boost by quickly learning to identify some of the colorful male ducks. But what about those female ducks, or winter-plumaged grebes and loons? And what about those males that we don't see very often or only at a distance or as a quick flyby? This book will help you identify these fascinating birds as well as learn a bit about their natural history.

What about those males that we don't see very often or only at a distance or as a quick flyby?

When trying to identify birds it is important to remember the following motto: *I don't know.*

Really, it's OK to say it. Too many birders will get an inconclusive view of a bird and then just guess. With practice, you can identify birds from incredibly short glimpses of them, but there will always be some "I don't knows." And even if you do get a good look and still can't identify the bird, you will have learned from the process. The next time you see that species, it will be familiar to you and you may see another field mark or behavior to help in its identification. And don't forget to watch the birds as well! Keeping a checklist is fun and a way to record your sightings, but careful observations will help you really understand these interesting creatures. Watching birds in their environment reveals interactions that link all of nature together.

FAIRBAIRN

How to use this book

= SWIMMING

A description of field marks to help identify swimming (or sitting) waterfowl. Words in *italics* are especially important identification features.

FIRST FALL/ FIRST WINTER

Birds that have not reached their adult plumage. Females usually look like the adults, but many first-fall or first-winter male ducks look similar to adult females.

ECLIPSE

This often dull plumage usually occurs during the early summer. Adult male ducks in this plumage have finished breeding and abandoned the females who incubate the eggs and raise the young. Eclipse males are usually very shy and secretive at this time. They have molted all their flight feathers, and so are temporarily flightless.

= IN FLIGHT

A description of field marks to help identify flying waterfowl. Often describes the wing and belly patterns.

LISTEN FOR

What common sounds the waterfowl species makes. Many species have more calls for courtship displays, but these are not usually included in this book. Please refer to the many good bird-sound tapes and CDs that are available.

COMPARE TO

This lists birds that look similar to the particular waterfowl species. At the back of the book you will find comparison pages. These will be helpful for comparing similar species.

SEASONAL STATUS

This list (pages 16–17) refers to the seasonal status of waterfowl at Point Pelee National Park, Ontario. Because Point Pelee is a fairly central point for Eastern North America, you can use this information as a guideline for when these birds may arrive or leave your area. However, because Point Pelee may not have the breeding or wintering habitat required for certain species, the application of this chart during the summer and winter may be less accurate.

The box at the top left of the page graphically represents the adult male's left upperwing pattern (see below).

SMALL

The full shoulder and speculum are graphically represented to help you note various wing patterns.

RANGE MAPS These maps show each species' breeding and wintering ranges, as well as where the species may be resident all year long.

A note to beginners

Watch the bird for a while before flipping through this guide.

WHEN LOOKING AT WATERFOWL, resist the urge to flip through this guide. Watch the bird first. This way you can look for field marks and behaviors before the bird disappears from your view. Ask yourself questions such as *Does it float high or low in the water? Is it diving (submerging) or dabbling (feeding at the surface)? What wing markings are there? What beak shape does it have? Is it hanging out with any other similarly shaped birds that have more distinctive field marks?*

After answering these and other questions, then look in this book. Waterfowl can be easily spooked or move into dense vegetation, and you should spend your time looking at them before they move on.

Try to learn the common species of your area first. Don't just learn the markings, but learn the shapes and flight patterns, too. Being familiar with shape, size, behavior and movements of common waterfowl species such as Mallards and Canada Geese will help with identification of the migratory or less common species that you will come across.

The quotes

SOME OF THE DESCRIPTIONS in this book include a quotation from naturalist writings on bird behavior and identification. Although these observations may seem unscientific or "fluffy" to some readers, I believe that these naturalists have a magnificent understanding of birds and their lives. Assigning human characteristics to nonhuman creatures (anthropomorphism) is unscientific, but I believe that beginners can benefit from this practice. What better way for a human being to learn about something than to use humanlike descriptions? So read the quotations, and then watch a duck doing its courtship display or listen to a loon calling. You may find that the melodramatic or colorful style does indeed apply to your subject.

What better way for a human being to learn about something than to use humanlike descriptions?

Taxonomy

THE WORD "WATERFOWL" is usually used to cover only ducks, swans and geese, but I use it here in more general terms to be able to cover other "ducklike" birds. Thus, many of the birds in this book are not very closely related; but all have adapted to swimming for a living.

All birds in this book have adapted to swimming for a living.

The order of the birds in this book follows the seventh edition and its supplements of the *American Ornithologists' Union Check-list of North American Birds*. The birds are arranged in a specific sequence (taxonomic order) that recognizes relationships between species. You may notice that many closely related birds, such as the *Anas* ducks, will have similar behaviors, shapes and flight patterns (see page 13). This will help you to use shape and behavior as identification aids while you learn something about taxonomic relationships among birds.

Classification

HERE IS A LIST that shows how the birds in this book are classified. Each genus in a family is listed to show which species are quite closely related.

Class Aves: Birds
Order Anseriformes: Ducks, Swans, Geese & Screamers
FAMILY ANATIDAE: DUCKS, SWANS & GEESE

Subfamily *Anserinae*: Swans & Geese
Genus	*Anser*	Greater White-fronted Goose
	Chen	Snow & Ross' Geese
	Branta	Brant, Canada & Cackling Geese
	Cygnus	Mute, Trumpeter & Tundra Swans

Subfamily *Anatidae*: Ducks
Genus	*Aix*	Wood Duck
	Anas	Gadwall, wigeons, American Black Duck, Mallard, teals, Northern Shoveler & Northern Pintail
	Aythya	Canvasback, Redhead, Ring-necked Duck & scaups
	Somateria	King & Common Eiders
	Histrionicus	Harlequin Duck
	Melanitta	Surf, White-winged & Black Scoters
	Clangula	Long-tailed Duck
	Bucephala	Bufflehead & goldeneyes
	Lophodytes	Hooded Merganser
	Mergus	Common & Red-breasted Mergansers
	Oxyura	Ruddy Duck

Order Gaviiformes: Loons
FAMILY GAVIIDAE: LOONS
| Genus | *Gavia* | Red-throated & Common Loons |

Order Podicipediformes: Grebes
FAMILY PODICIPEDIDAE: GREBES
Genus	*Podilymbus*	Pied-billed Grebe
	Podiceps	Horned, Red-necked & Eared Grebes
	Aechmophorus	Western Grebe

Order Pelecaniformes: Boobies, Pelicans, Cormorants and Allies
FAMILY PELECANIDAE: PELICANS
| Genus | *Pelecanus* | American White Pelican |

FAMILY PHALACROCORACIDAE: CORMORANTS
| Genus | *Phalacrocorax* | Double-crested Cormorant |

Order Gruiformes: Cranes, Rails and Allies
FAMILY RALLIDAE: RAILS
| Genus | *Gallinula* | Common Moorhen |
| | *Fulica* | American Coot |

Waterfowl groups

WATERFOWL CAN BE DIVIDED into general groups that have similar shapes or behaviors. Looking for these characteristics can help in field identification. Here are a few examples. Others are discussed in the text for each species.

Dabbler

Dabblers (Wood Duck & *Anas* ducks)
Though capable of diving, dabblers rarely submerge their whole bodies. They are often seen feeding on the surface by dabbling (opening and shutting their beaks on the water surface to filter out tiny organisms) or tipping up (dunking the front half of their bodies while their legs and tail go into the air). Overall, these birds float high on the surface of the water. They are able to walk easily on land because their legs are centrally located under their bodies. They can also rise from the surface of the water without needing a running start.

Diver

Divers (*Aythya* ducks, Eiders, Scoters, Long-tailed Duck, *Bucephala* ducks & Ruddy Duck)
These ducks usually feed by diving underwater. They tend to sit low on the water surface. They have trouble walking on land because their feet are placed toward the rear of their bodies. Most also need to take a running start to be able to take off.

Merganser

Mergansers
These ducks have the same characteristics as divers (above) – but they also have long thin beaks with toothed edges to aid in catching fish.

Grebe

Loons and Grebes
These diving birds have pointed beaks. Their feet are placed well to the rear of their bodies and they run along the water surface to get airborne. Loons have thick necks and long bodies, and they sit fairly low in the water. Grebes are more variable and tend to have thinner, longer necks and shorter bodies than loons.

Identification features

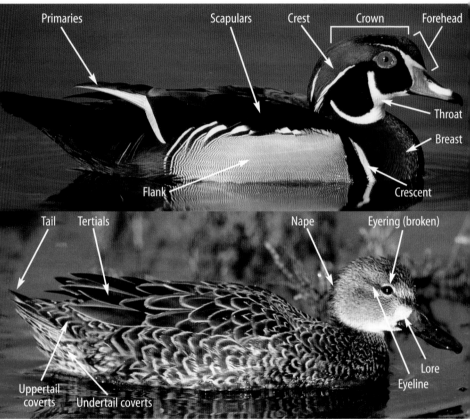

Primaries · Scapulars · Crest · Crown · Forehead · Throat · Breast · Flank · Crescent

Tail · Tertials · Nape · Eyering (broken) · Uppertail coverts · Undertail coverts · Lore · Eyeline

TOP: McCAW · BOTTOM: SMALL

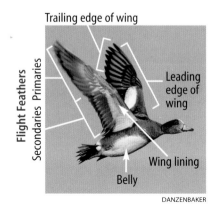

Trailing edge of wing · Leading edge of wing · Flight Feathers · Secondaries Primaries · Wing lining · Belly

DANZENBAKER

Speculum · Back · Shoulder or upperwing coverts

SMALL

Waterfowl look-alikes

OTHER SPECIES NOT COVERED in this book may swim on the water surface, so birders should be aware of them as well.

SMALL

Gulls (such as the Ring-billed shown here) often swim and can be mixed in with other waterfowl species.

SMALL

Phalaropes (such as the winter-plumaged Red-necked shown here) often feed by swimming in tight circles on the surface of the water. They are a species of shorebird or sandpiper.

SMALL

Aquatic seabirds, such as murres (shown here), puffins, dovekies, boobies and gannets, are usually restricted to saltwater habitats.

SMALL

Rails, such as this Sora, are closely related to the Common Moorhen and the American Coot and can sometimes be seen swimming.

You should also be wary of uncommon ducks in your area – sometimes birds escape from zoos or waterfowl parks. They often, but not always, have bands on their legs, but these can be hard to see. As well, some domestic ducks and geese may escape from farms and even mate with wild species to produce young with strange plumages.

Seasonal status of waterfowl
for Point Pelee National Park

■ **Common** ▒ **Uncommon** —— **Rare** ····· **Very rare**

Month	J	F	M	A	M	J	J	A	S	O	N	D
Fulvous Whistling-Duck 124												
Gr. White-fronted Goose 18												
Snow Goose 20												
Ross's Goose 22												
Canada/Cackling Goose 24												
Brant 26												
Mute Swan 28												
Trumpeter Swan 30												
Tundra Swan 32												
Wood Duck 34												
Gadwall 36												
Eurasian Wigeon 38												
American Wigeon 40												
American Black Duck 42												
Mallard 44												
Blue-winged Teal 46												
Garganey 125												
Cinnamon Teal 48												
Northern Shoveler 50												
Northern Pintail 52												
Green-winged Teal 54												
Canvasback 56												
Redhead 58												
Ring-necked Duck 60												
Tufted Duck 62												
Greater Scaup 64												
Lesser Scaup 66												
King Eider 68												
Common Eider 72												
Harlequin Duck 76												
Surf Scoter 78												
White-winged Scoter 80												
Black Scoter 82												

■ Common   **▓ Uncommon**   **— Rare**   **····· Very rare**

Month	J	F	M	A	M	J	J	A	S	O	N	D
Long-tailed Duck 84												
Bufflehead 88												
Common Goldeneye 90												
Barrow's Goldeneye 92												
Hooded Merganser 94												
Common Merganser 96												
Red-breasted Merganser 98												
Ruddy Duck 100												
Red-throated Loon 102												
Pacific Loon 127												
Common Loon 104												
Pied-billed Grebe 106												
Horned Grebe 108												
Red-necked Grebe 110												
Eared Grebe 112												
Western Grebe 114												
American White Pelican 116												
Great Cormorant 129												
Double-crested Cormorant 118												
Purple Gallinule 129												
Common Moorhen 120												
American Coot 122												

FROM J.R. GRAHAM 1996

Anser albifrons

Adult

THE GREATER WHITE-FRONTED GOOSE has one of the widest ranges of any goose species, breeding in much of northern Asia as well as northern North America. These geese migrate with fewer stops than others, allowing them to get to their breeding grounds quite quickly. Fewer stops as well as a mostly western range means they are not a common sight in the Great Lakes region during migration.

ADULT
Brown head and body • *white patch around the base of the beak* • pink beak • *black blotches on belly* • thin white line on upper flank • white undertail coverts • dark tail with a white tip • orange legs and feet.

FIRST WINTER
Similar to adult except for • yellowish beak • no white around the base of the beak • no white line on flank • no black blotches on belly • yellowish legs and feet.

ADULT
Brown head and body • gray on upperwing coverts • *black blotches on belly* • white undertail coverts • dark tail with white tip • white uppertail coverts.

Adults   McCAW

🦅 FIRST WINTER

Similar to adult except for • no black blotches on belly.

LISTEN FOR

A laughing *loo-laa-luck*.

COMPARE TO

First-winter blue morph of the Snow Goose, Brant.

NATURE NOTES

Unlike most other Arctic geese, Greater White-fronted Geese do not nest in colonies. These geese resemble some domestic geese such as graylags, so identification must be done carefully. May hybridize with Snow Goose or Canada Goose.

RANGE
Breeding only
Wintering only

19

White and blue adults

FLYNN

HUNDREDS OF THESE GEESE flying together really convey why their name is so appropriate – they look like a flurry of snowflakes. But they're very noisy snowflakes; the sound that these flocks make is an experience in itself. A huge flight of Snow Geese is something that everyone should see (and hear) at least once in their lifetime.

WHITE MORPH ADULT

All-white body and head · may have yellowish staining on head and neck · pinkish beak with *black "lips"* · *black wingtips* · pinkish legs and feet.

BLUE MORPH ADULT

Similar to white morph adult except for · dark gray body and lower neck with variable amount of white on underparts and wings · white tail.

WHITE MORPH FIRST WINTER

Dull light gray body and head · underparts whitish · dusky beak, legs and feet · faint eyeline.

BLUE MORPH FIRST WINTER

Grayish brown body and head · dusky beak, legs and feet · variable amounts of white on undertail coverts, belly and tail.

WHITE MORPH ADULT

All-white head and body · black primaries.

Adults, white and blue morph · SMALL

✈ BLUE MORPH ADULT

Dark gray body · white head · *variable white on neck* · variable white on belly, undertail coverts and tail · white wing linings · dark primaries and secondaries · lighter gray upperwing coverts.

✈ WHITE MORPH FIRST WINTER

Light gray body and head · dark gray primaries.

✈ BLUE MORPH FIRST WINTER

Dark grayish brown body and head · lighter gray upperwing coverts.

LISTEN FOR

A yelping *wuk*.

COMPARE TO

Ross's Goose, Greater White-fronted Goose.

NATURE NOTES

The blue morph of the snow goose was once thought to be a separate species called the "Blue Goose." Be wary of all-white geese that may be barnyard escapees.

White and blue first winters · SMALL

RANGE
◼ Breeding only
◻ Wintering only

21

Chen rossii

Adult

LOOKING LIKE A MINIATURE SNOW GOOSE, the Ross's Goose's smaller size and lack of "black lips" help differentiate it. The Ross's Goose also has a rare blue morph, but it is thought that this is due to hybridizing with the blue morph of the Snow Goose. The Ross's Goose population has increased from only 2,000–3,000 birds in the early 1950s to approximately 200,000 in the early 1990s.

ADULT
Small size • white head and body • short neck compared to most geese • pink beak • black primaries • pink legs and feet.

FIRST WINTER
Similar to adult except for • grayish cap, eyeline and back • dusky beak, legs and feet.

ADULT
White head and body • relatively short neck • *black primaries.*

FIRST WINTER
Similar to adult except for • grayish cap and back.

LISTEN FOR
A yelp, higher-pitched than the Snow Goose.

Adult Ross's with a Snow Goose

SMALL

COMPARE TO
Snow Goose.

NATURE NOTES
The nesting grounds for the Ross's Goose weren't found until 1940.

Adult and first winters

DANZENBAKER

RANGE

- ■ Breeding only
- ▨ Wintering only

Branta canadensis & Branta hutchinsii

Adult Canada Goose

"…WHAT MAN SO BUSY that he will not pause and look upward at the serried ranks of our grandest wildfowl … a harbinger of spring or a foreboding of winter. Certainly the Canada goose commands respect." This was written by Arthur Cleveland Bent in 1925. The Canada Goose population has expanded enormously since then, and today this goose can be watched all year in many areas. Although they're a common sight, these birds still present an impressive picture when a large flock graces the sky.

ADULT

Black head and neck • white cheek patch • black beak • brown body • light brown breast • dark primaries • white undertail coverts • black tail • black legs and feet.

ADULT

Black head and neck • white cheek patch • brown body • white undertail and uppertail coverts • dark primaries and secondaries • black tail.

LISTEN FOR

A loud *uh-ronk* by the males and a high-pitched *uh-rink* by females.

Adult Canada Geese

FLYNN

COMPARE TO

Brant.

NATURE NOTES

Canada Geese once showed the widest range of size and shape differences of any bird species in the world. The weight of adults ranged from only 3.5 pounds (1.6 kg) in some subspecies to 10.8 pounds (4.9 kg) in others. Because of these size differences and other morphological features, as of July 2004 there are now two species of these geese. The large subspecies are called Canada Geese and the smaller subspecies are called Cackling Geese. These may be split into even more species in the future.

Canada Geese are very defensive of their nests and goslings. I've seen an adult fly up and crash into a Red-tailed Hawk that was diving to grab a gosling, successfully stopping the potential predator.

IRON

Cackling Geese (shown here) are not as common in the east as Canada Geese

RANGE

- ■ Breeding only
- ■ Resident year round
- ■ Wintering only

Branta bernicula

Adult

BRANT ARE SMALL, DARK GEESE that favor saltwater habitats. They are among the fastest flying of geese, with some being recorded at reaching speeds of between 50 and 62 miles (80–100 km) an hour. "…they make a trumpetlike noise, which, heard at a distance, is said to resemble that of a pack of harriers or fox-hounds in full cry" (Studer, 1881).

ADULT

Black head, neck and breast • black beak • *white necklace* • brownish gray body • *some white edging on flanks* • dark primaries • short black tail • white undertail coverts • black feet and legs (western birds darker overall).

FIRST FALL

Similar to adult except for • no white necklace • no white on flanks • white edges on upperwing coverts.

ADULT

Black head, neck and breast • brownish gray body • *white edging on flanks* • white undertail coverts • white uppertail coverts • short black tail.

FIRST FALL

Similar to adult except for • no white edging on flanks • white edges on upperwing coverts.

Adult

DANZENBAKER

LISTEN FOR

A low *ronk*.

COMPARE TO

Canada Goose, Cackling Goose, first-winter blue morph of the Snow Goose.

NATURE NOTES

One study found that 15% of Brant nests were located near Snowy Owl nests. The geese benefit from the aggressive nest defense tactics of their owl neighbors, who keep potential predators such as Arctic Foxes away from the area.

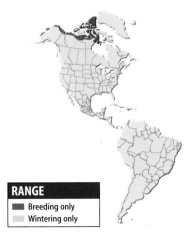

RANGE	
■	Breeding only
■	Wintering only

Cygnus olor

Adult

THIS SWAN HAS BEEN INTRODUCED to North America many times since the mid-1800s and is now a common breeder in some parts of the Great Lakes region and along the Atlantic coast. It does not tolerate intruders in its territory, and so it aggressively displaces other native waterfowl species. The negative effects of the Mute Swan's increasing population have prompted eradication efforts in some areas of its range.

First year   FAIRBAIRN

ADULT

All-white head, neck and body • head and neck may have a yellowish or rusty stain • *reddish orange beak with black knob* • light to dark legs and feet • *neck often kept in more of a curve than other swans.*

FIRST FALL

Similar to adult except for • grayish overall • dusky pink beak with no black knob.

Adult

McCAW

🦢 ADULT

All-white head, neck and body • *reddish orange beak with black knob* • tail longer and more pointed than other swans.

🦢 FIRST FALL

Similar to adult except for • grayish overall • dusky pink beak with no black knob.

LISTEN FOR

Grunts, hisses, snorts and a feeble honk; not really "mute," but not as loud as the other swans.

Adult

McCAW

COMPARE TO

Trumpeter Swan, Tundra Swan.

NATURE NOTES

The name for a male swan is a "cob." The name for a female swan is a "pen."

RANGE

▨ Resident year round

Cygnus buccinator

Adult   McCAW

"THE TRUMPETER HAS SUCCUMBED to incessant persecution in all parts of its range, and its total extinction is now only a matter of years … in the ages to come, like the call of the whooping crane, they will be locked in the silence of the past." Lucky for us, Forbush's (1912; in Bent) prediction has yet to come true. Though still very rare in the east, the Trumpeter Swan is being reintroduced to areas in the Great Lakes region and free-flying birds can be seen.

First year   McCAW

ADULT

All-white head, neck and body • head and neck may have yellow or rusty stain • large all-black beak (with a straight or slightly curved base • black feet and legs.

FIRST SPRING

Similar to adult except for • a grayish wash on head, neck and back • may have some dusky pink on beak.

Adult McCAW

FIRST FALL

Similar to first spring except for • more overall brownish gray wash on head, neck and body • dusky pink on beak • legs may be dusky pink.

ADULT

All-white head, neck and body • fairly short, rounded tail.

FIRST SPRING

Similiar to adult except for • a grayish wash on head, neck and body.

FIRST FALL

Similar to first spring except for • more overall brownish gray wash.

LISTEN FOR

A low-pitched honk or trumpet; more like a crane than a goose.

COMPARE TO

Tundra Swan, Mute Swan.

NATURE NOTES

The Trumpeter Swan is considered to be the heaviest of all flying birds, with some males weighing over 30 pounds (13.5 kg).

McCAW

Adult – note the line from the eye to the bottom of the beak is fairly straight and smooth

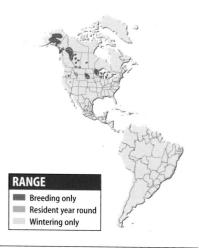

RANGE
- Breeding only
- Resident year round
- Wintering only

Adults and first years

SMALL

BECAUSE THE CANADA GOOSE is now common in much of eastern North America all year, it has lost its "harbinger of spring" status. But the graceful flight of the Tundra Swan has filled the position to announce that spring is indeed on its way. Much of the Tundra Swan's Atlantic coast wintering population passes through the Great Lakes region. This route gives many northeast birders a chance to see the long lines of flying Tundras or an agricultural field covered in a white of swans.

ADULT

All-white head, neck and body • black beak (with a curved, irregular base) • beak usually, but not always, has a yellow spot on lore • black legs and feet.

FIRST SPRING

Similar to adult except for • a slight grayish wash to head, neck and back • may have some dusky pink on beak.

FIRST WINTER

Similar to first spring except for • brownish gray wash on head, neck and body • mostly dusky pink beak • dusky pink legs and feet.

ADULT

All-white head, neck and body • short rounded tail.

Adult · FLYNN

▼ FIRST SPRING

Similar to adult except for • some grayish wash on head, neck and body.

▼ FIRST WINTER

Similar to first spring except for • more overall brownish gray wash on head, neck and body.

LISTEN FOR

A bark-like *who*; more like a goose than a crane.

COMPARE TO

Trumpeter Swan, Mute Swan.

NATURE NOTES

On the breeding grounds, nesting adults can usually fight off all predators except wolves, bears and humans.

McCAW

Adult – note the line from the eye to the bottom of the beak is more irregular and vertical than Trumpeter

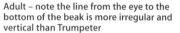

RANGE	
■	Breeding only
■	Wintering only

Aix sponsa

Breeding male

"THAT DUCK WAS ALL JEWELS combined, showing different lustres as it turned on the unrippled element in various lights, now brilliant glossy green, now dusky violet, now a rich bronze, now the reflections that sleep in the ruby's grain" (Thoreau, 1855). Yes, the male Wood Duck is about as ornate as possible. And it was once in decline over much of its range. Conservation efforts have now allowed this duck species to show its beauty again in much of eastern North America.

BREEDING MALE

Green head with *long, white-bordered crest* • red eyes • *reddish orange beak with white and black on top* • white throat with one white mark leading through cheek and one white mark leading partially around the neck • chestnut breast with small white specks • white crescent on side of breast • blue/purple on upperwing coverts and back • yellowish brown flanks • chestnut undertail coverts • *long tail* • orange legs and feet.

ECLIPSE MALE

Similar to female except for • white markings on throat, cheek and neck • red eyes • colorful beak.

ADULT FEMALE

Brown head and body • white patch around eye • dark beak • white throat

Adult female   SMALL

Eclipse male   FAIRBAIRN

• grayish brown flanks with light brown spots.

![] BREEDING MALE

Large headed and long tailed • head raised above body line • white throat with white markings on cheek and neck • chestnut breast • yellowish brown flanks • white belly • chestnut undertail coverts • blue speculum with white trailing edge • blue on some upperwing coverts • mottled gray underwing.

![] ADULT FEMALE

Large headed and long tailed • head raised above body line • brown head and body • white patch around eye • white throat • grayish brown flanks • white belly • blue speculum with white trailing edge.

LISTEN FOR

Male has a squeaky whistle that rises in pitch. Female has a loud *ooeeeek*.

COMPARE TO

Female Hooded Merganser.

NATURE NOTES

"Egg-dumping," where a female lays one or more eggs in another female's nest, is a common occurrence in many duck species. Wood Ducks usually have 10–15 eggs in a clutch, but because of egg-dumping, some nests may end up with more than 30 eggs – way too many for a female to incubate successfully.

RANGE
▇ Breeding only
▇ Resident year round
▇ Wintering only

Anas strepera

Breeding male SMALL

AT A DISTANCE, Gadwalls seem to be a very drab species, especially when compared to most of the other "gaudy" male dabbling ducks. But on close inspection, the male is quite striking, with his herringbone patterned breast feathers and black rear end. The female Gadwall nests in tall vegetation, often on islands. Because the nests are so well hidden, Gadwalls often have a higher rate of success in hatching young than do other duck species.

Adult female SMALL

⬛ BREEDING MALE

Fairly large grayish head • *steep forehead* • *black beak* • dark gray breast with light edges to feathers, giving a *herringbone or scaled appearance* • brownish gray back and flanks • brown scapulars • may show a bit of the *white speculum* • *black undertail and uppertail coverts* • gray tail • yellow legs and feet.

Male in flight   DANZENBAKER

Female in flight   DANZENBAKER

ECLIPSE MALE

Similar to female.

ADULT FEMALE

Steep forehead • mottled brown head and body • fairly faint eyeline • orange beak with black on top • may show a bit of the *white speculum*.

BREEDING MALE

Dark gray breast • brownish gray back and flanks • *white belly* • *gray wings with chestnut and black upperwing coverts* • inner part of *speculum is white*, outer part is black • white wing linings • *black undertail and uppertail coverts* • gray tail.

ADULT FEMALE

Mottled brown head and body • *white belly* • gray wings with some black upperwing coverts • inner part of *speculum is white*, outer part is dark gray.

LISTEN FOR

Females give a harsh quack.

COMPARE TO

American Wigeon, other female dabbling ducks (see comparison pages 132–33).

NATURE NOTES

Other names for the Gadwall include creek duck, gray wigeon, red-wing and speckle-belly.

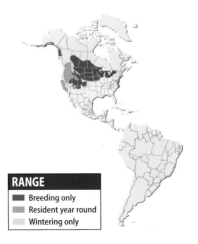

RANGE

■ Breeding only
■ Resident year round
□ Wintering only

Anas penelope

Breeding male

THE EURASIAN WIGEON's breeding range covers most of Asia and northern Europe, making it one of the most widespread of ducks in the Old World. In North America, however, this species is a rare find, though it has regular wintering grounds on the west coast. Still, the Eurasian Wigeon can show up almost anywhere, and there are records of it all over the continent.

Adult female flapping   DANZENBAKER

🦆 BREEDING MALE

Fairly large, round, *chestnut head flecked with white* • *steep, buffy yellow forehead* • light gray beak bordered with black • black tip on beak • purplish brown breast • light gray flanks and back • *white line of upperwing coverts* may be seen above flank • *white patch between flanks and undertail coverts* • black undertail and uppertail coverts • dark legs.

Adult female

DANZENBAKER

ECLIPSE MALE

Similar to female except for • a richer brown overall • may show the white of the upper-wing coverts as a line above the flank.

ADULT FEMALE

Fairly large, round, grayish brown head • *steep forehead* • *may have a dark patch around eye* • light gray beak bordered with black • black tip on beak • brownish body, *less distinctly mottled than other female dabbling ducks* • mottled undertail and uppertail coverts.

BREEDING MALE

Buffy yellow forehead • brownish breast • gray flanks • white belly • black undertail and uppertail coverts • *white upperwing coverts* • green speculum bordered with black • *gray wing linings*.

ADULT FEMALE

Brownish breast and flanks • white belly • mottled undertail and uppertail coverts • green speculum bordered with black • gray wing linings.

LISTEN FOR

Male has a loud 3-parted whistle. Female has a harsh *errrr*.

COMPARE TO

American Wigeon, Gadwall and other female dabbling ducks (see comparison pages 132–33).

NATURE NOTES

This species has not been recorded to nest in North America, though hybrids with American Wigeon have been seen.

Anas americana

Breeding male

THE AMERICAN WIGEON'S BEAK is shaped differently from that of other dabbling ducks. It is shorter and thicker, making it strong enough for this duck to graze like a goose. Wigeons have another feeding specialty – piracy. As noted by Studer (1881), the Canvasback possesses "superior powers of diving," but "… the Widgeon watches this duck until it brings to the surface the tender roots of the water-celery, when it instantly filches the dainty morsel and appropriates it to its own use." The American Wigeon will also steal from Redheads, Lesser Scaup and American Coots and has been seen to rob muskrats as well.

🦆 BREEDING MALE

Fairly large, round, *gray head flecked with white* • *steep, white forehead* • *green patch leading back from eye* • light gray beak bordered with black • black tip on beak • purplish brown breast and flanks • grayish brown back • *white line of* *upperwing coverts* may be seen above flanks • *white patch between flanks and undertail coverts* • black undertail and uppertail coverts • dark legs.

🦆 ECLIPSE MALE

Similar to female except for • may show a whitish forehead and a green patch

Adult female
SMALL

Male and female
DANZENBAKER

around eye • may show the white of the upperwing coverts as a line above the flank.

ADULT FEMALE

Fairly large, round, grayish brown head flecked with white • steep forehead • may have a dark patch around eye • light gray beak bordered with black • black tip on beak • brownish body, less distinctly mottled than other female ducks • mottled undertail and uppertail coverts.

BREEDING MALE

Green patch leading back from eye • white forehead • brownish breast and flanks • white belly • black undertail and uppertail coverts • white upperwing coverts • green speculum bordered with black • *center of wing linings white.*

ADULT FEMALE

Brownish breast and flanks • white belly • mottled undertail and uppertail coverts • *white bar on upperwing coverts* • green speculum bordered with black • *center of wing linings white.*

LISTEN FOR

Male has a loud 3-parted whistle with a "rubber duck" quality. Female has a harsh *errrr.*

COMPARE TO

Eurasian Wigeon, Gadwall and other female dabbling ducks (see comparison pages 132–33).

NATURE NOTES

Because of its habit of stealing food, another name for this duck is "poacher."

RANGE
Breeding only
Resident year round
Wintering only

American Black Duck

Anas rubripes

Breeding male · FLYNN

ONCE THE COMMON WOODLAND DUCK of the east, the American Black Duck has seen its population decrease quite dramatically since the mid-1950s. American Black Duck numbers have declined due to many factors, including the loss of breeding habitat. The clearing of forests has also invited the open-loving Mallard from the west to move eastward. These Mallards as well as farm-raised Mallards released for hunting purposes are hybridizing with the American Black Duck, creating another threat to their overall numbers.

ADULT MALE

Light brown head and neck · dark eyeline · *greenish yellow beak* · *dark brown body, contrasting with lighter neck and face* · orange legs.

ADULT FEMALE

Similar to male except for · dusky green beak · slightly lighter brown overall.

ADULT MALE

Light brown head and neck · *dark brown body, contrasting with lighter neck and face* · *purple speculum bordered with black* · *white wing linings, contrasting with dark flanks.*

ADULT FEMALE

Similar to male.

Breeding male showing speculum – note its dark contrast to the female Mallard behind it   FLYNN

Black Duck/Mallard cross   McCAW

White wing linings contrast with   DANZENBAKER
dark underparts and flight feathers

LISTEN FOR

Male has a raspy *reeb*. Female has a loud quack.

COMPARE TO

Other female dabbling ducks (see comparison pages 132–33).

NATURE NOTES

This species has a higher tolerance for salt than the Mallard, allowing it to utilize salt marshes and coastal islands for nesting purposes.

RANGE
- Breeding only
- Resident year round
- Wintering only

Anas platyrhynchos

Breeding male   McCAW

THIS IS THE MOST ADAPTABLE and, thus, the most abundant of all the ducks of North America. Even cities seem to offer habitat for this species, with females nesting in planters and under ornamental shrubs in downtown areas. And although the Mallard is commonly seen, many birders don't stop to notice it. If, however, you do take the time to study the shape and patterns of the female Mallard, you will, through comparison, be on your way to figuring out the other female dabbling ducks.

Female   McCAW

BREEDING MALE

Green head • *white neck ring* • yellow beak • *chestnut breast* • light gray back and flanks • black undertail and uppertail coverts • white outer tail and *curled black central tail feathers* • reddish orange legs.

ECLIPSE MALE

Similar to female except for • *dull yellow beak* • richer brown breast.

Eclipse male   FLYNN

🦆 ADULT FEMALE

Light brown head and neck · dark eyeline
· orange beak with dark patch on top
· mottled brown body · whitish tail.

🦆 BREEDING MALE

Green head · *white neck ring* · *chestnut breast* · light gray flanks and belly · black undertail and uppertail coverts · black rump · white outer tail and black central tail feathers · blue *or purplish speculum with white leading and white trailing edge* · white wing linings.

🦆 BREEDING FEMALE

Light brown head and neck · mottled brown body · whitish tail · *blue or purplish speculum with white leading and trailing edges* · white wing linings.

LISTEN FOR

Male has a raspy *reeb*. Female has a loud quack.

COMPARE TO

Northern Shoveler and other female dabbling ducks (see comparison pages 132–33).

Male   FLYNN

Female   FAIRBAIRN

NATURE NOTES

The female Mallard will sometimes place her nest right beside a nesting female Canada Goose and thus be protected from nest predators by the male goose.

RANGE

- Breeding only
- Resident year round
- Wintering only

Anas discors

McCAW

Breeding male

THE SWIMMING FEMALE BLUE-WINGED TEAL seems to typify the drab, mottled brown look of most female dabbling ducks. But when she springs into flight, the drabness is replaced by blue upperwing coverts. These blue patches are usually easy to see and are also present on the larger Northern Shoveler and the very similar Cinnamon Teal. The Blue-winged Teal is a long-distance migrant, often flying all the way to northern South America.

Adult female SMALL

BREEDING MALE

Purplish gray head and neck • *white crescent on face between eye and beak* • black beak • spotted brown breast and flanks • *white patch between flanks and undertail coverts* • black undertail and uppertail coverts • *yellow legs and feet.*

ECLIPSE MALE

Similar to female except for • may show hint of facial crescent.

Adult female – note yellow legs   DANZENBAKER

Breeding male   FLYNN

ADULT FEMALE

Brown head • dark eyeline • *whitish lore and throat* • dark beak • mottled brown body • *yellow legs*.

BREEDING MALE

Purplish gray head and neck • *white crescent on face between eye and beak* • spotted brown breast and flanks • white wing linings with dark leading edge • *blue upperwing coverts with a white trailing edge* • green speculum bordered with black • white patch between flanks and undertail coverts • black undertail coverts.

ADULT FEMALE

Brown head • mottled brown body • white wing linings with dark leading edge • *grayish blue upperwing coverts with a white trailing edge* • green speculum bordered with black.

LISTEN FOR

Male has high-pitched whistles or chirps (sometimes like a House Sparrow). Female has a high-pitched quack.

COMPARE TO

Other female dabbling ducks (see comparison pages 132–33).

NATURE NOTES

A Brown-headed Cowbird once laid an egg in a Blue-winged Teal nest (oops!). Blue-winged Teal are among the earliest ducks to migrate south in the fall and one of the latest ducks to return north in the spring.

RANGE

- Breeding only
- Resident year round
- Wintering only

Anas cyanoptera

Breeding male

THE CINNAMON TEAL IS a western bird, but it does show up occasionally in the east. In fact, there are even breeding records for this species in the Great Lakes region. The male Cinnamon Teal is an easy bird to identify with its reddish chestnut plumage, but the female looks very similar to the female Blue-winged Teal. These two species are closely related and sometimes hybridize. The breeding range of the Cinnamon Teal includes parts of South America.

Adult female   DANZENBAKER

BREEDING MALE

Bright reddish chestnut head and body • red eyes • black beak • black undertail and uppertail coverts • yellow legs and feet.

ECLIPSE MALE

Similar to female except for • red eyes • richer brown overall.

Adult female — DANZENBAKER

Breeding male — DANZENBAKER

ADULT FEMALE

Brown head • indistinct eyeline • *light lore* • large dark beak • *mottled brown body* • yellow legs.

BREEDING MALE

Bright reddish chestnut head and body • white wing linings with dark leading edge • blue upperwing coverts with a white trailing edge • green speculum bordered with black • black undertail coverts.

ADULT FEMALE

Brown head • mottled brown body • white wing linings with dark leading edge • *grayish blue upperwing coverts with a white trailing edge* • green speculum bordered with black.

LISTEN FOR

Male has a high-pitched whistle. Female has a high-pitched quack.

COMPARE TO

Other female dabbling ducks, especially Blue-winged Teal (see comparison pages 132–33).

NATURE NOTES

The Latin name *cyanoptera* means "blue wing."

RANGE

- ■ Breeding only
- ▨ Resident year round
- ▢ Wintering only

Anas clypeata

Breeding male

WHAT A SCHNOZ! The beak of the Northern Shoveler shows the adaptation of dabbling to its fullest. Many dabbling ducks strain small food items from the water by using comblike projections called lamellae. These lamellae are densest in the Northern Shoveler, allowing it to strain out smaller invertebrates than other dabblers. Northern Shovelers usually feed by dabbling at the surface of the water, but they sometimes tip up, too.

Adult female SMALL

🦆 BREEDING MALE

Green head and neck • yellow eye • *large black beak* • *white breast* • *rusty-chestnut flanks* • white between flanks and undertail coverts • black undertail and uppertail coverts • white tail • orange feet.

🦆 ECLIPSE MALE

Similar to breeding male except for • head, breast and flanks heavily mottled

Male eclipse · FAIRBAIRN

Males and a female · SMALL

with brown · *thin white crescent on face* · only small amounts of green on head.

ADULT FEMALE

Brown head · *large orange beak with black on top* · mottled brown body · orange legs.

BREEDING MALE

Green head and neck · *white breast* · white wing linings with thin dark leading edge · *blue upperwing coverts with white trailing edge* · green speculum bordered with black · *rusty-chestnut flanks and belly* · white between flanks and undertail coverts · black undertail coverts · white tail.

ADULT FEMALE

Brown head · large orange beak with black on top · mottled brown body · white wing linings with thin dark leading edge · *gray upperwing coverts with white trailing edge* · green speculum bordered with black.

LISTEN FOR

Female has a low-pitched, often 2-parted hollow quack.

COMPARE TO

Mallard and other female dabbling ducks (see comparison pages 132–33).

NATURE NOTES

Other names for this duck include broadbill, scooper, shovel-bill and spoonbill.

RANGE
■ Breeding only
■ Resident year round
■ Wintering only

Anas acuta

Breeding male

SMALL

"THE PINTAIL IS A GRACEFUL SWIMMER, riding lightly on the surface, with its tail pointing upwards, its general attitude suggestive of a swan and with its long neck stretched up, alert to every danger, the first to give the alarm and always the first of the shy waterfowl to spring into flight" (Bent, 1923). The male Northern Pintail is the most elegant of the dabbling ducks, and its slim long neck and pointed tail are shown subtly on the female as well.

Adult female

SMALL

BREEDING MALE

Dark chocolate brown head and upper neck • white stripe on hind neck • gray beak with black on top • white breast and lower neck • gray back and flanks • white patch between flanks and undertail coverts • black undertail and uppertail coverts • *long, black central tail feathers* • gray legs.

Breeding male   DANZENBAKER

Female   DANZENBAKER

ECLIPSE MALE

Similar to female except for • more white in neck • gray and black beak.

ADULT FEMALE

Brown head • rather plain face • longish neck • dark gray beak • mottled brown body • longish pointed tail • gray legs.

BREEDING MALE

Dark chocolate brown head and upper neck • white stripe on hind neck • *longish neck* • white breast and lower neck • *green speculum with a buffy leading edge and a white trailing edge* • gray wing linings, whitish in the center • gray back and flanks • white belly • white patch between flanks and undertail coverts • black undertail and uppertail coverts • *long, black central tail feathers*.

ADULT FEMALE

Brown head • longish neck • *bronze speculum with a buffy white leading edge and a white trailing edge* • gray wing linings, whitish in the center • mottled brown body • whitish belly • *longish tail*.

LISTEN FOR

Male has a double whistle. Female has a soft quack.

COMPARE TO

Other female dabbling ducks (see comparison pages 132–33).

NATURE NOTES

The Northern Pintail has been known to "play dead" when grabbed by a fox, likely in hopes of escaping when the predator's guard is down.

RANGE

■ Breeding only
■ Resident year round
■ Wintering only

Breeding male

THE GREEN-WINGED TEAL is found across the northern hemisphere, though the males of Europe and Asia differ a bit in appearance compared to our North American birds. The white crescent on the side of the breast of our teal is replaced by a white line on the scapulars of the Eurasian birds. Among the tiniest of ducks, they can be mistaken for a flock of shorebirds when they are seen in flight at a distance.

Adult female

SMALL

BREEDING MALE

Bright chestnut head and neck • *large head* • *steep forehead* • black beak • *large green patch leading backward from the eye* • buffy breast covered with black spots • white crescent on side of breast • gray flanks and back • yellow patch on black undertail coverts • gray or dusky yellow legs.

ECLIPSE MALE

Very similar to female.

Male between eclipse and breeding   McCAW

Adult female – note gray legs   McCAW

Male   DANZENBAKER

ADULT FEMALE

Brown head · *steep forehead* · indistinct eyeline · short dark beak · mottled brown body · buffy patch sometimes noticeable on undertail coverts · *gray legs*.

BREEDING MALE

Bright chestnut head and neck · large green patch leading backward from the eye · buffy breast covered with black spots · *green speculum with buffy leading edge and thin white trailing edge* · dark gray wing linings with white in center · pale belly · white crescent on side of breast · gray flanks and back · yellow patch on black undertail coverts.

ADULT FEMALE

Brown head · mottled brown body · *green speculum with buffy leading edge and thin white trailing edge* · dark gray wing linings with white in center.

LISTEN FOR

Male may whistle (sometimes sounds like a spring peeper). Female has a high-pitched quack, sometimes in a descending series.

COMPARE TO

American Wigeon, Blue-winged Teal and other female dabbling ducks (see comparison pages 132–33).

RANGE

■ Breeding only
■ Resident year round
■ Wintering only

55

Breeding male

SMALL

I LIKE THE NAME "door-stop duck" for this species because its head is so sloped and angular that it looks like the wedge you'd use to keep a door open. This head shape should help you separate the Canvasback from its close look-alike, the Redhead. Canvasbacks often unwittingly provide food for other waterfowl by bringing vegetation to the surface after their dives. Mallards, American Wigeons, Northern Pintails, Gadwalls, Ruddy Ducks and American Coots have all been seen to gather this floating vegetation around Canvasbacks.

BREEDING MALE

Reddish chestnut head and neck • wedge-shaped head • red eyes • long black beak • black breast • grayish white back and flanks • black undertail and uppertail coverts • dark legs.

ECLIPSE MALE

Similar to breeding male, but duller and browner overall.

ADULT FEMALE

Brown head and breast • *wedge-shaped head* • dark eye • black beak • indistinct whitish eyeline behind eye • brownish gray back and flanks • dark legs.

BREEDING MALE

Reddish chestnut head and neck • black breast • grayish white back and flanks • white wing linings • upperwing coverts

Adult female

SMALL

and speculum with lots of grayish white
• black undertail coverts.

ADULT FEMALE

Brown head and breast • brownish gray
back and flanks • white wing linings
• brownish gray upperwing coverts and
speculum.

LISTEN FOR

Female has a low growl.

COMPARE TO

Redhead (see comparison page 134),
female Ring-necked Duck.

NATURE NOTES

The Canvasback is a very fast flying duck
that is able to reach speeds of over 60
miles (100 km) an hour.

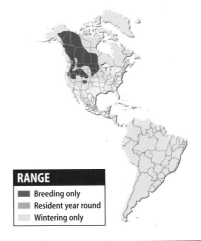

RANGE
- ■ Breeding only
- ▩ Resident year round
- ▢ Wintering only

Aythya americana

Breeding male

THE FEMALE REDHEAD is the queen of nest parasitism. Redheads have been known to lay their eggs in the nests of more than 10 other duck species, as well as the nests of other birds such as American Bitterns, American Coots, Soras and even Northern Harriers! Their favorite host species are Canvasbacks and other Redheads. In some areas, 100 percent of Canvasback nests may be parasitized by Redheads.

BREEDING MALE

Bright reddish chestnut head and neck • *gray beak with white ring and black tip* • *yellow eye* • black breast • gray back and flanks • black uppertail and undertail coverts.

ECLIPSE MALE

Similar to breeding male, but duller and browner overall.

ADULT FEMALE

Brown head and body • *gray beak with faint whitish ring and black tip* • dark eye • indistinct whitish eyeline behind eye.

BREEDING MALE

Bright reddish chestnut head and neck • *black breast* • gray back and flanks • white wing linings • gray upperwing coverts • lighter gray speculum • black undertail coverts.

Adult female

SMALL

Breeding male

McCAW

Adult female

FLYNN

ADULT FEMALE

Brown head and body • brownish upperwing coverts • light gray speculum.

LISTEN FOR

Female has a growling squawk.

COMPARE TO

Canvasback (see comparison page 134), female Ring-necked Duck.

NATURE NOTES

Redheads sometimes have a "dump nest," where different females lay eggs but no one usually incubates them. In one case, however, a female tried to incubate 44 eggs! Only one egg hatched.

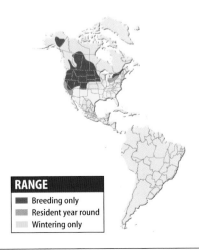

RANGE	
■	Breeding only
■	Resident year round
■	Wintering only

Aythya collaris

Breeding male

THIS GORGEOUS DUCK has the best from both worlds. It's a diving duck, and therefore can dive well. But unlike other diving ducks, this species can take off from the water without a running start. It's also quite quick and maneuverable in the air, sometimes compared to flying teals. The male Ring-necked Duck does indeed have a ring around its neck, but this faint band of chestnut is hard to see. The ring around its beak suggests a better name.

Adult female SMALL

BREEDING MALE

Black head with purplish sheen • head has a peaked shape • yellow eye • *gray beak with white outline at base, white ring at end and black tip •* chestnut collar hard to see • *black breast and back • white crescent on side of breast •* gray flanks • black undertail and uppertail coverts and tail.

Eclipse male   SMALL

Males and females   McCAW

🦆 ECLIPSE MALE

Similar to breeding male except for
• duller overall • less distinct beak
markings • brownish flanks.

🦆 ADULT FEMALE

Brown head • *head has a peaked shape*
• brown eye • *brownish gray cheeks* (gives
the bird a bit of a capped appearance)
• white at the base of the beak • white
eyering • *white eyeline behind eye* • *gray
beak with white ring and black tip* • brown
breast and flanks • darker brown back,
undertail and uppertail coverts (female
may be browner overall in the summer).

🦆 BREEDING MALE

Black head • black breast and back • white
belly • gray flanks • grayish underwings
• black upperwing coverts • *gray speculum*
• black undertail and uppertail coverts
and tail.

🦆 BREEDING FEMALE

Brown head, breast and back • brownish
gray cheeks • white belly • brown flanks
• grayish underwings • *brown upperwing
coverts* • *gray speculum* • brown undertail

and uppertail coverts and tail.

LISTEN FOR

Female has a soft growl.

COMPARE TO

Scaups, female Redhead (see comparison
pages 146–47).

NATURE NOTES

This species isn't a picky eater, so it can
often nest in bogs and other inhospitable
places that other ducks may avoid.

RANGE

■ Breeding only
▦ Resident year round
□ Wintering only

Tufted Duck

Aythya fuligula

Breeding male

THE TUFTED DUCK ranges across Europe and Asia, but is sometimes seen in North America, including the Great Lakes region and the Atlantic coast. The male's long tuft of head feathers, when seen, is a distinctive field mark and he can be separated from the similar scaup by his black back. The female looks a lot like female scaup, so she can be hard to distinguish in the field.

BREEDING MALE

Black head with a purplish sheen • *long tuft of feathers hanging from the back of the head* • yellow eye • gray beak with a whitish ring and a black tip • *black breast and back* • *white flanks* • black uppertail and undertail coverts • black tail.

ECLIPSE MALE

Similar to breeding male except for • duller overall • brownish flanks • little or no tuft.

ADULT FEMALE

Dark brown head, breast and back • *small crest* not always easy to see • sometimes white at the base of the beak • gray beak with a whitish ring and black tip • brownish gray flanks.

BREEDING MALE

Black head and upperparts • white flanks and belly • white underwings • black upperwing coverts • *white speculum and into the primaries*, all with a black trailing

Adult female

edge • black uppertail and undertail coverts • black tail.

ADULT FEMALE

Brown head and upperparts • white flanks and belly • white underwings • brown upperwing coverts • *white speculum and into the primaries*, all with a dark trailing edge • black uppertail and undertail coverts • black tail.

LISTEN FOR

Female has a low growl.

COMPARE TO

Ring-necked Duck, Lesser and Greater Scaup (see comparison pages 146–47).

NATURE NOTES

This species may hybridize with scaup, so identification of some individuals can be tricky.

Male

Aythya marila

Breeding male

McCAW

THE GREATER AND LESSER SCAUP offer the biggest challenge in identification of any of the duck species, and both the males and the females are difficult to tell apart. Head shape is a very important characteristic for distinguishing these species. But depending on the duck's "mood," even this characteristic can be unreliable. It is important to note that not all scaup can be identified conclusively. Remember, it is OK to say "I don't know."

BREEDING MALE

Black head, often with a greenish sheen (but could be purple) • *head is rounded with the highest point often in front of the eye* • gray beak with black tip • black breast • white flanks • gray back • black undertail and uppertail coverts.

ECLIPSE MALE

Similar to breeding male except for
• duller overall • brownish flanks and back

• may show a trace of white at the base of the beak.

ADULT FEMALE

Brown head and breast • *head is rounded with the highest point often in front of the eye* • white at the base of the beak (less white in first-year females) • gray beak with black tip • may have whitish patch on ear (more common in summer) • grayish brown back and flanks.

Adult female

SMALL

 BREEDING MALE

Black head and breast • white flanks and belly • gray back • light gray underwings • gray upperwing coverts • *white speculum that goes into the primary feathers*, all with a black trailing edge • black undertail coverts.

 ADULT FEMALE

Brown head and breast • may see a white patch at the base of the beak • brown flanks • white belly • brown back • light gray underwings • brownish gray upperwing coverts • *white speculum that goes into the primary feathers*, all with a black trailing edge.

LISTEN FOR

Female has a low growl.

COMPARE TO

Lesser Scaup (see comparison page 135), Ring-necked Duck.

NATURE NOTES

Greater Scaup are usually larger and look chunkier than Lesser Scaup.

Eclipse male

McCAW

RANGE

■ Breeding only
☐ Wintering only

Aythya affinis

Breeding male

McCAW

WHEREAS THE GREATER SCAUP breeds in the tundra throughout the northern hemisphere, the Lesser Scaup is found only in North America. Like the Greater Scaup, these ducks will often form very large flocks on their wintering grounds. When both scaup occur together in one large flock, each species may still be found in separate groupings.

BREEDING MALE

Black head, often with a purplish sheen (but could be green) • *head is peaked with the highest point often behind the eye* • gray beak with black tip • black breast • white or light gray flanks • gray back • black undertail and uppertail coverts.

ECLIPSE MALE

Similar to breeding male except for • duller overall • brownish flanks and back • may show a trace of white at the base of the beak.

ADULT FEMALE

Brown head and breast • *head is peaked with the highest point often behind the eye* • white at the base of the beak (less white in first-year females) • gray beak with black tip • may have whitish patch on ear (more common in summer) • grayish brown back and flanks.

BREEDING MALE

Black head and breast • white (or grayish) flanks and belly • gray back • light gray underwings • gray upperwing coverts

Adult female
FAIRBAIRN

Female in summer
SMALL

· *white speculum that does not usually go into the gray primary feathers*, all with a black trailing edge · black undertail coverts.

ADULT FEMALE

Brown head and breast · may see a white patch at the base of the beak · brown flanks · white belly · brown back · light gray underwings · brownish gray upperwing coverts · *white speculum that does not go into the gray primary feathers*, all with a black trailing edge.

Adult male, flapping – note bright white in secondaries only
SMALL

LISTEN FOR

Female has a low growl.

COMPARE TO

Greater Scaup (see comparison page 135), Ring-necked Duck.

NATURE NOTES

While the amount of white in the flight feathers is one of the best field marks for distinguishing the two scaup species, as many as 9% of individuals may overlap and thus not be identifiable by this characteristic.

RANGE

■ Breeding only
░ Resident year round
░ Wintering only

Somateria spectabilis

Breeding male

"THE MOST STRIKINGLY BEAUTIFUL of all the Arctic birds is undoubtedly the male King Eider. His regal plumage warrants fully his royal name" (W.E. Ekblaw; in Bent, 1925). A good look at a male King Eider will certainly prove this to be true to any observer. Low-flying lines of King Eiders with the landscape of Baffin Island in the background is one of my most cherished Arctic memories. But a trip to the Arctic isn't always needed to see one, as King Eiders are sometimes found in winter in the Great Lakes region or along the Atlantic coast.

BREEDING MALE

Bluish gray cap and nape • white bordered black eyeline • white cheek with greenish wash • *bright yellowish orange knob on beak, bordered with black* • bright orange beak • white throat and neck • white breast washed with buff • white upper back • black lower back and flanks • two black "shark fins" sticking up from back (not always easy to see) • white line between back and flanks • white patch between flanks and undertail and uppertail coverts • black undertail and uppertail coverts • black tail.

ECLIPSE MALE

Dark brown head and body with some

Adult female

FLYNN

mottling • *orange beak with a slight knob* • white line between back and flanks • white "V" on back • whitish patch between flanks and tail.

FIRST-WINTER MALE

Similar to eclipse male except for • whiter breast • no "V" on back • less of a knob on beak • duskier beak

ADULT FEMALE

Brown head and body • *indistinct buffy eyeline and eyering* • black beak • body mottled • *flanks have sideways "Vs"* • sometimes shows small white patch in wing just above flank.

BREEDING MALE

Bluish gray cap and nape • black eyeline • white cheek, neck and breast • *bright yellowish orange knob on beak, bordered*

RANGE

Breeding only
Wintering only

first-winter male

FLYNN

with black • bright orange beak • white upper back • black lower back, flanks and belly • white upperwing coverts with black leading edge on all-black wing • white wing linings contrasting with dark flight feathers • white patch between flanks and undertail and uppertail coverts • black undertail and uppertail coverts • black tail.

FIRST-WINTER MALE

Similar to breeding male in flight except for • all black replaced with dark brown • dark brown head • lack of knob on beak • dusky underwings.

ADULT FEMALE

Brown head and body • body mottled • brownish underwing with white center • brown upperwing coverts • dark speculum with a thin white leading and a thin white trailing edge.

LISTEN FOR

Female growls; may give low croaks when flying.

COMPARE TO

Common Eider (see comparison page 146).

NATURE NOTES

The King Eider is one of the bird world's most northerly nesters.

Breeding male

DANZENBAKER

Adult female

McCAW

Somateria mollissima

Breeding male

THE COMMON EIDER is the largest duck in North America and is best known for its insulating down. The main predators of these Arctic-nesting ducks are Arctic Foxes, which may kill the nesting female as well as eat the eggs. This is especially common when the lemming population is low and if there are late ice bridges that allow the foxes to get to nesting islands. Another predator, the Polar Bear, can wipe out entire colonies of nesting Common Eiders.

First-winter male

BREEDING MALE

White head • *black cap* • *greenish gray or greenish yellow beak* • green wash on nape • white breast with a buffy wash • white back • two white "shark fins" sticking up from back (not always seen) • black flanks • black undertail and uppertail coverts • black tail.

Adult female

McCAW

ECLIPSE MALE

Very dark brown head and body with some whitish mottling on face and breast • *greenish gray or greenish yellow beak* • white line between flanks and back.

FIRST-WINTER MALE

Similar to eclipse male except for • grayer beak • white breast • variable white on back.

ADULT FEMALE

Brown head and body • gray beak • body mottled • *flanks and back are barred* (Hudson Bay and western females are grayer overall).

BREEDING MALE

White head • *black cap* • white breast and back • black flanks and belly • white wing linings and black flight feathers • white

RANGE
- Breeding only
- Resident year round
- Wintering only

Breeding males

DANZENBAKER

upperwing coverts and black flight feathers • black undertail and uppertail coverts • black tail.

▼ FIRST-WINTER MALE

Dark brown head, flanks, belly, uppertail and undertail coverts • white breast • dark brown wings.

▼ BREEDING FEMALE

Mottled brown head and body • *grayish underwings with white centers* • brown upperwing coverts • dark speculum with a thin white leading edge and a thin white trailing edge.

LISTEN FOR

Female growls.

COMPARE TO

King Eider (see comparison pages 146).

NATURE NOTES

These eiders can swallow whole mussels up to 2 inches long (5 cm).

Adult female

First-winter male

Breeding male

McCAW

THE FLASHY MALE HARLEQUIN DUCK has splashes of white spots and stripes on a slatey blue body plus a few chestnut highlights. As always with female ducks, the female Harlequin is much plainer, but she doesn't need racing stripes to prove that she, too, is at home in her breeding habitat. The Harlequin Duck is a bird of fast, clear rivers and is able to swim and dive in the seemingly dangerous currents to search for its prey.

BREEDING MALE

Dark bluish gray head and body • *white crescent on face* • *chestnut stripe on side of crown* • *white spot behind eye and a white oval behind that* • white stripe on neck • white crescent on side of breast • white patch above flank • white tertials • chestnut flanks • white spot on side of undertail coverts.

ECLIPSE MALE

Similar to female except for • whitish crescent on side of breast • whitish tertials (first-winter male is similar).

ADULT FEMALE

Brown head and body • irregular white patch at base of beak • *white spot behind eye.*

Adult female

SMALL

BREEDING MALE

Dark bluish gray head and body • *white crescent on face* • white spot behind eye and a white oval behind that • white stripe on neck • white crescent on side of breast • dark upperwings • some white spots on upperwing coverts • bluish speculum • dark wing linings and lighter flight feathers • *chestnut flanks and belly*.

BREEDING FEMALE

Brown head and body • irregular white patch at base of beak • white spot behind eye • dark upperwings • slight bluish speculum • dark wing linings and lighter flight feathers • white belly.

LISTEN FOR

Female has a harsh quack. Male may squeak. This call gave this species another name – the sea mouse.

COMPARE TO

Female Surf and White-winged Scoters, female Bufflehead (see comparison pages 148–49).

NATURE NOTES

One study on Harlequin Ducks found that many of the birds had mended fracture sites on different bones. Obviously riding the rapids can be hazardous.

RANGE

■ Breeding only
■ Wintering only

Surf Scoter

Melanitta perspicillata

Breeding male

SMALL

SKUNK-HEAD, BLOSSOM-BILLED COOT, Goggle-nose and Horse-head: these are all names that once described the Surf Scoter and its splendid appearance. At close range, the male is unmistakable due to the white patches on his head and his extraordinary beak. This scoter species is found only in North America, while the other two species are found here as well as throughout Europe and Asia.

BREEDING MALE

Black head and body • *white patches on forehead and nape* • *orange, yellow and white beak with a large black spot on the side* • white eye (first-spring male has no white patch on forehead).

ECLIPSE MALE

Similar to breeding male except for
• dusky brown overall (first-winter male is similar).

BREEDING FEMALE

Dark brown head and body • *beak forms a vertical line where it meets the face* • variable whitish patches at the base of the beak and behind the eye • eye pale • sometimes a whitish patch on the back of the head.

FIRST-SPRING FEMALE

Similar to breeding female except for
• larger white patches on face, giving

Female   SMALL

head a capped appearance • dark eye • no patch on nape.

▼ BREEDING MALE

Black head and body • *white patches on forehead and nape* • orange, yellow and white beak with a large black spot on the side • wings all black above • black wing linings with slightly lighter flight feathers

▼ BREEDING FEMALE

Dark brown head and body • variable whitish patches at the base of the beak and behind the eye • eye pale • sometimes a whitish patch on the back of the head • dark brown wings above and below.

LISTEN FOR

Female has a harsh quack.

COMPARE TO

White-winged and Black Scoter (see comparison pages 138–39).

NATURE NOTES

As a young birder, I once announced loudly at the local sewage lagoons: "Look, a flock of scooters!" It took a while to live that one down.

Breeding male   DANZENBAKER

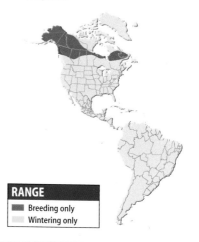

RANGE
Breeding only
Wintering only

White-winged Scoter

Melanitta fusca

Breeding male

McCAW

THIS IS THE "EASY" SCOTER to identify because of its white speculum. Even at a distance the white stands out, whether the birds are flying or if one does a wing stretch or flap while on the water. A female White-winged Scoter may nest far from water, so she might have to walk her newly hatched young a few miles to the nearest pond. That must be quite a challenging walk for a diving duck!

first-spring female

McCAW

BREEDING MALE

Black head and body • small white crescent under eye • white eye • orange beak with small black knob at base • may be able to see part of white speculum while swimming • brownish flanks may appear black at a distance (first-winter male duller overall and little or no crescent near eye).

ECLIPSE MALE

Similar to breeding male except for
• duller overall.

Males and females   McCAW

Male flapping   SMALL

ADULT FEMALE

Brown head and body • dark eye • whitish patches at base of beak and behind ear • lore area extends into the beak forming a curved line (first-spring females have larger whitish patches on face) • may be able to see part of the *white speculum*.

BREEDING MALE

Black head and body • black upperwing with large *white speculum* • black wing linings with white speculum and dark primaries • brownish flanks and belly (may appear black at a distance).

BREEDING FEMALE

Brown head and body • brown upperwing with large white speculum • brown wing linings with white speculum and dark primaries.

LISTEN FOR

A harsh quack.

COMPARE TO

Black Scoter and Surf Scoter (see comparison pages 138–39).

NATURE NOTES

In Europe, it is called the Velvet Scoter because of its black plumage.

RANGE

Breeding only
Wintering only

81

Black Scoter

Melanitta nigra

Adult male

DANZENBAKER

THE BLACK SCOTER is one of the least studied of North American birds, and very few nests have been found. The only confirmed breeding area in eastern North America is northern Quebec. The Black Scoter is well named, since the male is all black with his only flashy part being an orange knob on the base of his beak. The pale cheeks of the female make her easier to distinguish than the other female scoters.

Adult female

FLYNN

BREEDING MALE

Black head and body • orange knob on the base of the beak • round head.

ECLIPSE MALE

Similar to breeding male except for • slightly duller overall.

FIRST-WINTER MALE

Brown head and body • dull orange knob on beak • light brown patches near base of beak and behind eye.

Adult male

DANZENBAKER

ADULT FEMALE

Brown head and body • *light brown cheeks*.

BREEDING MALE

Black head and body • black upperwings • black wing linings with slightly lighter flight feathers

BREEDING FEMALE

Brown head and body • *light brown cheeks* • brown upperwings • brown wing linings with slightly lighter flight feathers.

LISTEN FOR

Female has harsh growls.

COMPARE TO

White-winged Scoter and Surf Scoter (see comparison pages 138–39).

NATURE NOTES

Some female scoters may abandon their young to fend for themselves as little as one week after they hatch.

RANGE	
■	Breeding only
■	Wintering only

Long-tailed Duck

Clangula hyemalis

Winter male

"OLDSQUAWS, OR LONG-TAILED DUCKS, as I should prefer to have them called, are lively, restless, happy-go-lucky ducks, known to most of us as hardy and cheery visitors to our winter sea coasts." A.C. Bent (1925) would be happy to know that the once-called Oldsquaw is now the Long-tailed Duck. These Arctic ducks are found in the Great Lakes region and along much of the Atlantic coast in the winter. Long-tailed Ducks have a distinctive breeding and winter plumage.

BREEDING MALE

Black head and body · *large white patch around eye* · black beak with pinkish spot on the top · brown scapulars · white flanks · white undertail coverts · *long, black central tail feathers.*

WINTER MALE

White head, neck and upper breast · *large gray cheek patch* · large black patch behind cheek · black beak with pinkish spot on the top · black lower breast · black back with white scapulars · white flanks and undertail coverts · black uppertail coverts · *long, black central tail feathers* (first-winter male duller overall).

BREEDING FEMALE

Brown head and body · *white patch around eye* · white eyeline behind eye and

Winter female

down to a partial ring around the neck
• dark gray beak • light brown foreflanks
blending to white undertail coverts.

WINTER FEMALE

White head and neck • brown cap and
nape • *brown patch below cheek* • dark
gray beak • brown breast and back • white
flanks and undertail coverts.

BREEDING MALE

Black head, back and breast • *large white
patch around eye* • brown scapulars • black
wing linings with slightly lighter flight
feathers • black upperwing with dark
brown speculum • white flanks and belly
• white undertail coverts • *long, black
central tail feathers*.

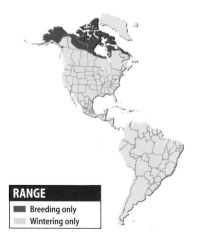

RANGE

■	Breeding only
▫	Wintering only

Winter male and female

DANZENBAKER

WINTER MALE

White head, neck and upper breast • *large gray cheek patch* • large black patch behind cheek • black lower breast • white flanks, belly and undertail coverts • black back with white scapulars • black wing linings with slightly lighter flight feathers • black upperwing with dark brown speculum • *long, black central tail feathers.*

BREEDING FEMALE

Brown head and body • white patch around eye • dark brown wing linings with slightly lighter flight feathers • dark brown upperwing with slightly lighter brown speculum • white belly and undertail coverts.

WINTER FEMALE

White head and neck • brown cap and nape • brown patch below cheek • brown breast and back • dark brown wing linings with slightly lighter flight feathers • dark brown upperwing with slightly lighter brown speculum • white belly and undertail coverts.

LISTEN FOR

Male has a loud, distinctive yodel *old-squawa-k.* Female has low quacks.

COMPARE TO

Female Bufflehead, female Wood Duck.

NATURE NOTES

This duck swims under water by using its partially folded wings and may not use its feet, unlike other diving ducks. This method allows the Long-tailed Duck to dive deeper than other species – over 200 feet (60 m).

Breeding male

Breeding female

Bucephala albeola

Breeding male

YES, THE BUFFLEHEAD IS CUTE. And its plucky nature and striking plumage have given it another name, as described by Bent (1925). "The propriety of applying the name 'spirit duck' to this sprightly little duck will be appreciated by anyone who has watched it in its natural surroundings, floating buoyantly, like a beautiful apparition, on the smooth surface of the pond or quiet stream … it seems indeed a spirit of the waters."

Adult female

BREEDING MALE

Black head with a rainbow of iridescence seen at close range in the right conditions • *large white patch that extends from behind the eye and includes the nape* • gray beak • white underparts • black back.

ECLIPSE MALE

Similar to female except for • larger white patch on head • may show a white line between flanks and back

Adult male   FAIRBAIRN

Adult female   SMALL

 ADULT FEMALE

Small brown duck • light brown underparts • *small white patch on cheek* • gray beak.

BREEDING MALE

Black head • large white patch on back of head • black back with a white line near wing • whitish wing linings and dark gray primaries • *white patch on upperwing coverts connects to white speculum* • white underparts.

BREEDING FEMALE

Dark brown head • white patch on cheek • light brown breast, flanks and undertail coverts • dark brown back • light brown wing linings with darker brown flight feathers • dark brown upperwing with white speculum.

LISTEN FOR

Female has a series of short croaks.

COMPARE TO

Common and Barrow's Goldeneyes, Hooded Merganser, female Long-tailed Duck.

NATURE NOTES

Buffleheads are so small that the females' preferred cavity nest sites are abandoned Northern Flicker holes.

RANGE	
■	Breeding only
■	Resident year round
□	Wintering only

Bucephala clangula

Breeding male

McCAW

THE COMMON GOLDENEYE has a spectacular courtship display that can be watched in late winter or early spring among the floating patches of ice. The male stretches out his head and then pulls it backward until it is resting on his back. He then gives a raspy call, throws his head forward and kicks out with his orange feet, sending up a spray of water. As with other duck species, there are many other courtship behaviors to watch for, too.

Adult female

McCAW

🦆 BREEDING MALE

Large, almost triangular, black head with a green iridescence • sloped forehead • large black beak • *yellow eye* • *circular white spot at the base of the beak* • white breast and flanks • black back • *white scapulars with some thin black stripes* • black undertail and uppertail coverts.

🦆 ECLIPSE MALE

Similar to female except for • all-black

First-year male — McCAW

beak • may show a white stripe between back and flanks.

FIRST-WINTER MALE

Similar to female except for • darker head • all-black beak • variable amount of white at base of beak.

ADULT FEMALE

Large, *almost triangular, brown head* • *yellow eye* • black beak with varying amounts of yellow on the tip (very rarely all yellow) • white collar (not always seen on resting birds) • gray body.

BREEDING MALE

Large black head • circular white spot at the base of the beak • white breast, flanks and belly • black back • white scapulars • black wing linings with slightly lighter flight feathers and white speculum • black leading edge on *white upperwing coverts that connect to white speculum* • black undertail and uppertail coverts.

BREEDING FEMALE

Large brown head • *white collar* • gray flanks and back • white belly • dark brown underwings and slightly lighter flight

feathers with white speculum • dark brown upperwing coverts with a white patch divided by a brown line plus a thin dark trailing edge • *white speculum.*

LISTEN FOR

Female has a low, harsh growl. The male's wings make a loud whistling sound when in flight, giving this duck another name, "Whistler."

COMPARE TO

Barrow's Goldeneye (see comparison page 140), Bufflehead.

NATURE NOTES

Some fish such as Yellow Perch compete with Common Goldeneyes for food sources; so much so that the goldeneyes may avoid lakes that have these fish in them. In fact, Common Goldeneyes actually do well in areas that have been affected by acid rain, which lowers fish populations.

RANGE
- Breeding only
- Resident year round
- Wintering only

Bucephala islandica

Breeding male

THOUGH IT BREEDS in greater numbers in western North America, the only confirmed breeding site for the Barrow's Goldeneye in the east is southeastern Quebec. During the winter, most eastern birds are found at the mouth of the St. Lawrence River, though smaller numbers may be seen along the Atlantic coast and the in Great Lakes region. The female goldeneyes can be hard to tell apart; here is another example of where shape rather than field marks is most useful.

Adult female SMALL

BREEDING MALE

Large, *blockish, black head* with a purple iridescence • *steep forehead* • often a bulge at the nape, making the head look very long and wide • black beak • yellow eye • *crescent-shaped white spot at the base of the beak* • white breast and flanks • black crescent on side of breast • black back • *black scapulars with some small white spots* • black undertail and uppertail coverts.

ECLIPSE MALE

Similar to female except for • all-black beak • may show white spots on scapulars.

FIRST-WINTER MALE

Similar to female except for • darker head • all-black beak • variable amount of white at base of beak.

ADULT FEMALE

Large, blockish, brown head • *steep forehead* • often a *bulge at the nape*, making the head look very long and wide • mostly yellow beak with some black • yellow eye • white collar (not always seen on resting birds) • gray body.

BREEDING MALE

Large black head • crescent shaped spot at the base of the beak • white breast and flanks • black back • black scapulars with some small white spots • black wing linings with slightly lighter flight feathers and white speculum • *white upperwing coverts with black leading and trailing edges separating them from the white speculum* • black undertail and uppertail coverts.

BREEDING FEMALE

Large brown head • white collar • gray flanks and back • white belly • dark brown underwings and slightly lighter flight feathers with white speculum • *dark brown upperwing coverts with a white patch and dark trailing edge* • white speculum.

LISTEN FOR

Female has a series of low growls. Male's wings give a whistling sound.

Eclipse male   SMALL

COMPARE TO

Common Goldeneye (see comparison page 140).

NATURE NOTES

Black Bears can be a common nest predator to this and other northern cavity-nesting ducks.

RANGE

- ■ Breeding only
- ▦ Resident year round
- ▢ Wintering only

Lophodytes cucullatus

FAIRBAIRN

Breeding male displaying

"THE MALE, WITH HIS SHOWY CREST and neat color pattern is one of the handsomest of our ducks, a fit companion for the gaudy wood duck with which it is often associated in the watery woodlands where it breeds" (Bent, 1923). More than having just an association, the Wood Duck and the Hooded Merganser compete for nesting cavities and are known to lay their eggs in each other's nests, as well as those of Common Goldeneyes and Common Mergansers.

Adult female

SMALL

BREEDING MALE

Large black head with long crest that can be raised dramatically • *white patch behind eye is bordered with black* • long, thin, black beak • *yellow eye* • black upper breast • white lower breast • two black crescents on the sides of the breast • black back • white lines on lower back • reddish chestnut flanks • black undertail and uppertail coverts.

Breeding male, crest down — McCAW

Breeding male — DANZENBAKER

ECLIPSE MALE

Similar to female except for • yellow eye • dark beak (first-winter male is similar – may have some black mottling on face).

ADULT FEMALE

Grayish brown head and body • *long thin beak, dark above, yellow below* • reddish chestnut crest.

BREEDING MALE

Large black head with long crest • white patch behind eye is bordered with black • long, thin, black beak • white breast and belly • two black crescents on the sides of the breast • black back • black upperwing with brownish patch on upperwing coverts • white wing linings and grayish flight feathers • black-and-white striped speculum • reddish chestnut flanks • black undertail and uppertail coverts.

BREEDING FEMALE

Grayish brown head and body • long thin beak • reddish chestnut crest • dark gray upperwing • black-and-white striped speculum • white belly.

LISTEN FOR

Female has a harsh croak; sometimes given in a series in flight.

COMPARE TO

Male Bufflehead, female Common and Red-breasted Mergansers (see comparison pages 140–41).

NATURE NOTES

The many predators on their eggs include Raccoons, Mink, Marten, bears, starlings, flickers, Red-headed and Red-bellied Woodpeckers and Black Rat Snakes.

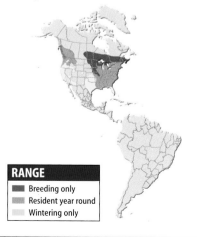

RANGE
■ Breeding only
▦ Resident year round
▧ Wintering only

Adult male

McCAW

THE MALE COMMON MERGANSER is a large, colorful duck that attracted Thoreau's attention many times. He wrote (1855), "I get sight of its long, slender, vermilion bill (color of sealing wax) and its clean, bright-orange legs and feet, and then its perfectly smooth and spotlessly pure white breast and belly, tinged with a faint salmon." The salmon tinge can be hard to see, especially at a distance, but is well worth looking for.

Adult female

FLYNN

BREEDING MALE

Dark green head (may appear black) • *long, thin, red beak* with a black line on top • dark eye • black back • white neck and underparts • breast may be washed with buffy-pink • reddish orange feet.

ECLIPSE MALE

Similar to female except for • may show a white stripe between the flanks and the back.

Breeding males in flight

DANZENBAKER

FIRST-WINTER MALE

Similar to female except for • some dark patches on head, especially around eye • may show more white between flanks and back.

ADULT FEMALE

Brown head with a crest • *clear line where brown of head meets gray of neck* • white chin patch • long, thin, orange beak • gray body • whitish on breast.

BREEDING MALE

Dark green head (may appear black at a distance) • long, thin, red beak • black back • white neck and underparts • white wing linings with dark primaries and white speculum • white patch on upperwing coverts partially divided by a black line from white speculum • reddish orange feet.

BREEDING FEMALE

Brown head with a crest • *clear line where brown of head meets gray of neck* • *white chin patch* • long, thin, orange beak • gray body • white wing linings with dark primaries and white speculum • gray

patch on upperwing coverts with dark trailing edge • white speculum • whitish on breast • white belly.

LISTEN FOR

Female has a harsh croak; sometimes given in a series in flight.

COMPARE TO

Red-breasted and Hooded Mergansers (see comparison page 141).

NATURE NOTES

This large duck prefers to nest in cavities, but sometimes nests on the ground.

RANGE	
■	Breeding only
▨	Resident year round
▨	Wintering only

Breeding male

McCAW

ANOTHER FASCINATING BREEDING DISPLAY to watch for is that of the male Red-breasted Merganser. These males point their beaks upward, then dip their breasts deeply into the water while the rear end of the bird is lifted out of the water. This display, called a "salute-curtsy," is done in small groups of males displaying for a female. The whole scene is accented by the males' punk hairdos and wide-open red eyes.

Adult female

SMALL

BREEDING MALE

Dark green head (can appear black) · *long crest*, often appears as two crests · long, thin, red beak · *red eyes* · white collar · *reddish brown breast* · black with white spots on the sides of the breast · gray flanks · black back bordered with white · white undertail coverts · gray uppertail coverts.

◁◀ ECLIPSE MALE

Similar to female except for • may show more white between flanks and back.

◁◀ FIRST-WINTER MALE

Similar to female except for • some dark patches on head • may show more white between flanks and back.

◁◀ ADULT FEMALE

Brown head • long crest, often appears as two crests • long, thin, orange beak • *whitish throat blending with gray of neck* • gray body.

First-year male   SMALL

◀ BREEDING MALE

Dark green head (can appear black at a distance) • white collar • *reddish brown breast* • white wing linings and speculum with dark primaries • white upperwing coverts with black leading edge • white upperwing covert patch joins white speculum but is divided by two dark lines • gray flanks • white belly • black back bordered with white • white undertail coverts.

Breeding male   DANZENBAKER

◀ ADULT FEMALE

Brown head • whitish throat blending with gray of neck • gray body • white belly • white wing linings and speculum with dark primaries • gray upperwing coverts, with white trailing edge joining white speculum divided by one dark line.

NATURE NOTES

The Red-breasted Merganser is a very fast flying duck that is able to reach speeds of up to 80 miles (130 km) an hour.

LISTEN FOR

Female has a harsh croak; sometimes given in a series in flight.

COMPARE TO

Common and Hooded Mergansers (see comparison page 141).

RANGE

■ Breeding only
□ Wintering only

Breeding male

McCAW

"WITH HIS SNUB-NOSED, belligerent profile and glowing colors, the ruddy duck is an engaging and delightful bird to see and never more so than when indulging in the elaborate courtship of his species. Then he is at his electric best…" Fenwick Lansdowne (1980) captured the Ruddy Duck not only in his paintings, but also in his description of the male's bizarre courtship display. The male inflates his neck and beats it rapidly with his bright blue beak while making a low clucking sound.

BREEDING MALE

Black cap • *white cheeks* • *bright blue beak* • *reddish chestnut body* • dark tail that may be held erect or flat on the water surface.

WINTER MALE

Dark brown cap • *white cheeks* • gray beak • grayish brown body • dark tail that may be held erect or flat on the water surface.

ADULT FEMALE

Dark brown cap • *white cheek divided by a brown line* • grayish brown body • dark tail that may be held erect or flat on the water surface.

BREEDING MALE

Black cap • *white cheeks* • bright blue beak • reddish chestnut body • whitish belly • mottled white wing linings with

Adult female

SMALL

dark flight feathers • upperwing coverts may have reddish chestnut coloration.

WINTER MALE

Dark brown cap • *white cheeks* • gray beak • grayish brown body • mottled white wing linings with dark flight feathers • brownish upperwing coverts and all-dark flight feathers.

ADULT FEMALE

Dark brown cap • *white cheek divided by a brown line* • grayish brown • mottled white wing linings with dark flight feathers • brownish upperwing coverts and all-dark flight feathers.

LISTEN FOR

Female has a nasal *aaaah*.

COMPARE TO

Female Bufflehead.

NATURE NOTES

This duck lays the biggest eggs for its body size of all of our ducks – each egg similar in size to that of a Wild Turkey. A nest of 7 eggs weighs approximately 96% of the female's body weight!

Winter male

FLYNN

RANGE

Breeding only
Resident year round
Wintering only

Red-throated Loon

Gavia stellata

Breeding adult

SMALL

THE SMALLEST OF THE LOONS, the Red-throated can be seen in the Great Lakes region as it migrates between its Atlantic coast winter grounds and its northern breeding grounds. Some may even winter on the Great Lakes. Unlike other loons, which need a long stretch of water to run along before they can take off, the Red-throated Loon can take off within a short distance and can even take off from the ground.

BREEDING

Gray head • striped nape • red throat • fairly thin beak that appears to turn slightly upward • white breast with stripes on sides • dark brownish-gray back.

WINTER

White head and neck with dark cap and nape • dark back with small white spots (not easy to see) • whitish flanks (first-year birds are similar but with gray necks).

BREEDING

Gray head • long pointed wings • dark upperwings • whitish underwings • dark back • white underparts.

WINTER

White head and neck with dark cap and nape • long pointed wings • dark upperwings • white underwings • dark back • white underparts.

Winter adult

SMALL

LISTEN FOR

A catlike wail and various other calls – may quack in flight.

COMPARE TO

Common Loon (see comparison page 142), Western Grebe, Red-necked Grebe.

NATURE NOTES

The Latin name *stellata* comes from the small white spots or "stars" found on this loon's winter plumage.

RANGE

■ Breeding only
▦ Resident year round
░ Wintering only

Common Loon

Gavia immer

Breeding adult

"MANY ORNITHOLOGISTS SPEAK of the voice as harsh and disagreeable; but the writer can not avoid confessing to a partiality for the loud mourning call of the Loon." Jacob Studer (1881) was obviously ahead of his time. Nowadays, the sound of the Common Loon means true wilderness to most of the people who hear its haunting cry. As well, the Common Loon is a great subject for behavior watchers, since its many actions and sounds convey different moods.

BREEDING

Black head and neck • long, pointed, *black beak* • red eyes • *white necklace* • white breast with thin black stripes on sides • black flanks and tail with small white dots • black back with large white squares • black feet.

WINTER

Brown head and neck • *white throat and chin blending with brown of neck*

• *suggestion of a white necklace* • *broken white eyering* • gray beak • white breast • brown body and tail (first year is similar to winter adult).

BREEDING

Black head, neck and back – may be able to see white squares • white breast, belly and undertail coverts • black flanks and tail • long pointed wings • black upperwing • white underwing • black back with white squares • black feet trail behind tail.

Winter adult

SMALL

WINTER

Brown head, neck and back • white throat and chin • white breast, belly and undertail coverts • brown flanks and tail • long pointed wings • brown upperwing • white underwing.

LISTEN FOR

A variety of hoots, wails, yodels, tremelos and laughs.

COMPARE TO

Red-throated Loon (see comparison page 142), Western Grebe, Common Merganser.

NATURE NOTES

The Common Loon will aggressively defend its territory not – only from other loons, but also from ducks, grebes, otters, beavers, raccoons and even snapping turtles. A group of loons has actually been seen attacking a swimming coyote. A loon may attack a duck by swimming under it and stabbing with its sharp beak, killing the duck instantly.

RANGE
■ Breeding only
☐ Wintering only

Pied-billed Grebe

Podilymbus podiceps

Breeding adult

THIS GREBE'S BEAK is different from that of other grebes because it is so short and thick. This strong tool is used to subdue one of its favorite prey species – the crayfish. The Pied-billed Grebe also eats fish, aquatic insects and even frogs. In the meantime, this small bird can become food for other animals, including reptiles such as Snapping Turtles and, in the south, American Alligators and Water Moccasins.

BREEDING

Brownish gray head and body • *black throat* • dark forehead • *white eyering* • dark eye • *strong, thick beak with a black ring near the tip.*

WINTER

Brownish gray head and body • whitish throat • dark eye • indistinct eyering • *strong, thick beak* (first-fall birds may have stripes on head).

BREEDING

Brownish gray overall • black throat • whitish belly • whitish trailing edge on secondaries • large feet trail behind.

WINTER

Brownish gray overall • whitish throat • white belly • whitish trailing edge on secondaries • large feet trail behind.

Winter adult

SMALL

LISTEN FOR

A song that is similar to that of the Yellow-billed Cuckoo – a series of cow notes that gradually slow down: *cow-cow-cow-cooow-coooow-cooowlp-cowlp-cowlp-cowlp*.

COMPARE TO

Winter-Eared Grebe, Horned Grebe (see comparison page 143).

NATURE NOTES

Pied-billed Grebe chicks have been observed to grab a parent's tail just before it dove, and were seen to be still holding it when the adult surfaced.

RANGE
- Breeding only
- Resident year round

Horned Grebe

Podiceps auritus

Breeding adult

SMALL

AS A YOUNG NATURALIST, I once found a Horned Grebe nest on the edge of a dugout on my uncle's farm. Even though the nest was quite exposed, the adult would sit still as if no one could see its bright golden horns. The fluffy, striped chick that hatched often received a piggyback ride on a parent, and it would snuggle under the adult's folded wings with only its head sticking out.

BREEDING

Large black head • *thick, golden eyebrow or "horns"* that go to the back of the head • red eyes • dark pointed beak with a small light tip • brownish lores • reddish chestnut neck, breast and flanks • gray back.

WINTER

White head and neck with dark cap and nape • smudgy gray on sides of neck • red eyes • gray pointed beak with a small light tip • reddish line joining eye to beak • gray back • whitish mottled flanks (first fall may be browner overall).

BREEDING

Black head • golden "horns" • reddish chestnut neck, breast and flanks • white belly • dark upperwings • white speculum • variable white patch on shoulder • whitish underwings with dark leading edge • large feet trail behind.

Winter adult

▼ WINTER

White head and neck with dark cap and nape • variable amounts of gray on neck • white breast and belly • dark upperwings • white speculum • variable white patch on shoulder • whitish underwings with dark leading edge • large feet trail behind.

LISTEN FOR

Trills and chatter; some high-pitched calls similar to gulls.

COMPARE TO

Eared Grebe, especially in winter (see comparison page 143).

NATURE NOTES

Many grebes eat large quantities of feathers – up to 66% of the stomach contents of a Horned Grebe may be its own feathers. It is thought that the feathers may help in the formation of pellets that are regurgitated to rid the stomach of indigestible food parts.

RANGE	
■	Breeding only
■	Wintering only

Podiceps grisegena

Breeding adult

McCAW

THE RED-NECKED GREBE is probably the most "loonlike" grebe because of its heavy beak, fairly thick neck and large size. Loons and grebes are often considered to be closely related because they have similar adaptations for being proficient divers. However, some studies show that loons may be more closely related to penguins or frigatebirds, and grebes may be more closely related to cormorants and anhingas.

BREEDING

Black cap and *grayish white cheek* • dark eye • long sharp beak, dark on top, yellowish underneath • reddish chestnut neck • brown body.

WINTER

Brownish gray overall • faint patch behind eye • *dark cap* • light yellow beak • reddish chestnut wash to neck • dark eye • long beak (first fall may have stripes on cheek).

BREEDING

Black cap • gray cheek • reddish chestnut neck • white belly • dark upperwing with white leading edge • white speculum • whitish underwing • large feet trail behind.

WINTER

Dark cap • light patch behind cheek • brownish neck • dark upperwing with white leading edge • white speculum

Winter adult

SMALL

• whitish underwing • large feet trail behind.

LISTEN FOR

A nasal grunting; also, wails, whinnies and rattles.

COMPARE TO

Horned Grebe, Eared Grebe and Red-throated Loon.

Flapping, showing speculum

FAIRBAIRN

NATURE NOTES

Like other grebes, the Red-necked Grebe may build platforms that are used only for copulation, not nesting.

RANGE

Breeding only
Wintering only

Podiceps nigricollis

Breeding adult

SMALL

STUDIES ON EARED GREBES revealed an interesting phenomenon. Because these grebes don't need to fly during incubation, raising of young, molting or staging for migration, they lose muscle mass in their flight muscles. This means that they are unable to fly for 9–10 months of the year. When they are ready for migration, their muscles build up quickly and become strong enough for long flights and their hearts even increase in size to help with their journey.

BREEDING

Black head and neck • long, thin, *yellow feathers radiating from behind the red eye* • head may be pointed on top • black, thin, pointed beak • *beak appears slightly turned up at tip* • brownish wash on black breast • brown flanks • black back.

WINTER

Black head • white chin • white patch behind cheek • gray, thin, pointed beak • *beak appears slightly turned up at tip* • *mostly dark neck* • white breast • dark back • whitish flanks (first fall may be browner overall).

BREEDING

Black head and neck • yellowish patch on cheek • brown flanks • white belly • dark upperwings • white speculum • whitish underwing with dark leading edge • large feet trail behind.

Winter adult

SMALL

▼ WINTER

Dark head and neck • white patch behind cheek • brownish flanks • white belly • dark upperwings • white speculum • whitish underwing with dark leading edge • large feet trail behind.

LISTEN FOR

A 3-parted whistle – *oooo-eeee-a, oooo-eeee-a.*

COMPARE TO

Horned Grebe, Pied-billed Grebe.

NATURE NOTES

Eared Grebes eat mostly small invertebrates. Before finishing their southward migration, they stop at salt lakes where they may eat up to 70,000 brine shrimp a day.

RANGE

■ Breeding only
■ Resident year round
■ Wintering only

Adult

McCAW

THE COURTSHIP DISPLAY of the Western Grebe is one of the most dramatic behaviors in the bird world. The display, called "rushing," is done by a male and female or two males and is characterized by both birds raising their bodies up out of the water, bending their necks and running along the surface together for up to 60 feet (18 m). At the end of the run, the two birds dive into the water and may continue with different displays when they surface.

ADULT

Black head and nape • white throat, lower cheek and neck • red eyes • long thin neck • long, sharp, yellowish beak • black body.

ADULT

Black head and nape • white throat, lower cheek and neck • long thin neck • long, sharp, yellowish beak • black back • white belly • dark upperwings with whitish at base of flight feathers • whitish underwing with dark "armpits" • large feet trail behind.

LISTEN FOR

A squeaky whistle and a 2-parted creak.

COMPARE TO

Red-throated Loon, Clark's Grebe.

A Western Grebe pair during their courtship display

McCAW

A pair "rushing"

McCAW

NATURE NOTES

This species once included the Clark's Grebe (see page 128) as a color variant, but it is now thought that the two are different species.

RANGE

- Breeding only
- Resident year round
- Wintering only

Pelecanus erythrorhynchos

Breeding adult

THE AMERICAN WHITE PELICAN has a huge wingspan – up to 9 feet (2.7 m). Seeing a flock of these magnificent birds flying overhead is a humbling experience. To match their extreme size, they also have gone to extremes with their beaks. These huge pouched structures are used to catch fish. Sometimes, flocks of swimming pelicans will work as a team to herd schools of fish toward shore for easier capture.

BREEDING

Very large • *white overall* • long neck • *extremely large orange beak* • hornlike projection from top of beak • orange legs and feet.

NON-BREEDING

Similar to breeding adult except for • no horn on beak • may have brownish wash on top of head near end of breeding season.

ADULT

Very wide wingspan • *white overall* • *extremely large orange beak* • neck tucked in • *black primaries and outer secondaries* • orange feet.

LISTEN FOR

Piglike grunts in the breeding colony.

COMPARE TO

Brown Pelican, swans.

116

Adult in flight

FLYNN

Adult in late summer

McCAW

NATURE NOTES

Though the average number of eggs laid in a nest is two, usually less than 10% of pairs raise both young. The younger chick often dies within the first two weeks of life.

RANGE

- Breeding only
- Wintering only

117

Double-crested Cormorant

Phalacrocorax auritus

Adult

REAUME

THE DOUBLE-CRESTED CORMORANT is a highly adaptable species and can be found foraging in many aquatic environments, such as open oceans, large lakes, slow rivers and even swamps. In recent years, this species has become very common in the Great Lakes region, even though contaminants in the lakes had previously caused the cormorants to have thin eggshells, crossed beaks and brain abnormalities.

Adult

SMALL

BREEDING

Black overall • black "horns" in north, white ones in south • *long, hooked, bright orange beak* • long neck • green eye • dark feet.

NON-BREEDING

Similar to breeding adult except for • duller overall • no "horns."

FIRST YEAR

Brown overall • pale throat and breast • long neck • long, hooked, orange beak.

First year

McCAW

ADULT

Black overall • long neck • orange beak.

FIRST YEAR

Brown overall • *pale throat and breast* • long neck • orange beak.

LISTEN FOR

Hoarse croaks and grunts in colonies.

COMPARE TO

Loons.

NATURE NOTES

The name *Phalacrocorax* is Greek and means "bald-headed raven."

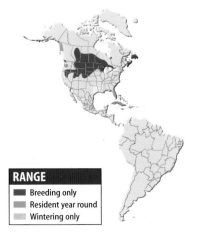

Adult and first years in flight

McCAW

RANGE	
■	Breeding only
■	Resident year round
■	Wintering only

Gallinula chloropus

Breeding adult   SMALL

REX BRASHER (1962) wrote that Common Moorhens "seem to me to be entirely lacking in that caution which enables most forms of wildlife to survive." It is amazing how tame these birds can be, and yet at times you can't see them at all. But you will still hear them. Brasher continues to note that "a freshwater marsh inhabited by one or more pairs of these birds is not a quiet spot."

Adult, showing feet   SMALL

🦆 BREEDING

Black head • pointed *red beak with shield on forehead* • yellow tip on beak • dark gray body • white stripe on flank • brown back • white patch on side of tail • yellow legs • *long toes*.

🦆 NON-BREEDING

Similar to breeding adult except for • duller red beak • whitish mottling on head and neck (first winter is similar but lighter overall and no red in beak).

First winter

FAIRBAIRN

🔻 ADULT

Black head • red beak • dark gray body • white patch on side of tail • brownish upperwing with thin, white leading edge • gray underwings • long legs and toes trail behind.

LISTEN FOR

A variety of loud whinnies, clucks, grunts and honks. American Coots sound very similar to Common Moorhens.

COMPARE TO

American Coot.

NATURE NOTES

When threatened, the Common Moorhen has been known to dive underwater and hide its bright red beak in vegetation. Though it doesn't have any webbing or lobes on its feet, the Common Moorhen can still swim quite well. Boardwalks through marshy areas give birders a wonderful opportunity to watch moorhens and other waterfowl.

RANGE
- Breeding only
- Resident year round

Fulica americana

Adult McCAW

THIS COMICAL BIRD is fun to watch as it moves its head in tune with its swimming or walking legs. To a territorial coot, however, the sight of an intruder of its own species is often too much to bear and could end in a battle of flailing feet. American Coots can be so aggressive that they have been known to evict many duck species from their territories, along with grebes, herons and shorebirds. Even small birds, snakes and turtles may be chased off.

Adult, showing feet   McCAW

ADULT

Black head • *pointed white beak with dark ring near tip* • red shield on forehead • reddish eye • dark gray body • small white patch on side of tail • greenish legs • *lobed toes*

Adult

DANZENBAKER

FIRST FALL

Pale brownish gray overall • darker on back • dark eye • pointed greenish beak • small white patch on side of tail • greenish legs • lobed toes

ADULT

Black head • white beak • dark gray body • dark wings with thin, white trailing edge on speculum • long legs and toes trail behind

LISTEN FOR

A variety of loud whinnies, clucks, grunts and honks. Common Moorhens sound very similar to American Coots.

COMPARE TO

Common Moorhen, Pied-billed Grebe

NATURE NOTES

Over a 3-day period in early spring 1931, approximately 10,000 coots were seen to migrate in a long flock. But they weren't flying – they were *walking* north!

RANGE
■ Breeding only
■ Resident year round
■ Wintering only

Vagrants and southern and coastal specialties

MOST OF THE FOLLOWING SPECIES are rare occurrences in eastern North America. Some, however, are regularly found in the south or on the Atlantic coast.

Black-bellied Whistling-Duck

Dendrocygna autumnalis

This tall, long-necked duck is a resident of southern Texas, but sometimes shows up in eastern North America. In flight, the Black-bellied Whistling-Duck is easy to identify because of its bold white wing stripe and dark flight feathers.

SMALL

Fulvous Whistling-Duck

Dendrocygna bicolor

A close relative of the Black-bellied Whistling-Duck, the Fulvous Whistling-Duck is plainer overall and has darker wings in flight. It can be regularly found along the Gulf coast and the southern half of Florida, but vagrants have been recorded all along the Atlantic coast as well as in inland parts of eastern North America.

SMALL

Barnacle Goose

Branta leucopsis

The Barnacle Goose is a bird of the
European Arctic, but sometimes strays to
eastern North America. Because this and
other waterfowl are often kept in
captivity, it can be very difficult to know if
a vagrant is a wild bird or an escapee.

SMALL

Mottled Duck

Anas fulvigula

This mallardlike duck is found along the
Gulf coast, along parts of the southern
Atlantic coast and throughout most of
Florida. It can be distinguished from the
female mallard by its yellower beak,
darker body and thinner white borders
on its speculum.

SMALL

Garganey

Anas querquedula

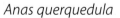

The Garganey is a duck of Europe, Asia
and Africa. The male is distinctive with his
long white eyebrow. The female, however,
is similar to the female Blue-winged Teal,
but has a more boldly striped face. This
species could turn up anywhere in North
America, but is rare.

FLYNN

Steller's Eider

Polysticta stelleri

This northerly bird breeds and winters in Alaska, but there are records of it farther south on both coasts of North America. Though it is an eider, its shape is much different from that of the other three species, and the male is the only one with flanks that aren't black.

FLYNN

Smew

Mergellus albellus

The Smew is a small merganser that lives in Europe and Asia where, like the Hooded and Common Merganser, it uses old woodpecker holes as nests. It is a very rare straggler to eastern North America.

FLYNN

Masked Duck

Nomonyx dominicus

This relative of the Ruddy Duck ranges from Mexico to central South America. It is quite shy, and so is hard to see even when it does show up farther north. It has been recorded from the Gulf coast northward to the Great Lakes region.

SMALL

A breeder over much of Arctic North America, the Pacific Loon usually winters on the west coast. It sometimes is seen in the Great Lakes region during migration and is also recorded along the Atlantic Coast in winter.

McCAW

Yellow-billed Loon

Gavia adamsii

The Yellow-billed Loon breeds in much of the central Arctic as well as the northern coast of Alaska. It usually winters along the west coast, but is sometimes seen in eastern North America.

DANZENBAKER

Least Grebe

Tachybaptus dominicus

This tiny grebe is found in southernmost Texas and southward, though it has traveled farther east on a few occasions. Its small size, bright yellow eye and thin beak help to distinguish it from other grebes.

SMALL

Clark's Grebe

Aechmophorus clarkii

Once thought to be the same species as the Western Grebe, the Clark's Grebe ranges farther west. The white surrounding its eye is the best way to distinguish it from the Western.

SMALL

Brown Pelican

Pelecanus occidentalis

The Brown Pelican is easy to distinguish from the larger American White Pelican (it's brown, not white!). The Brown Pelican also hunts differently, often plunge-diving headfirst from the air into the surface of the water. It is found all along the southern coasts, but sometimes strays to the Great Lakes region and as far north as Canada's Maritime Provinces.

FLYNN

Neotropic Cormorant

Phalacrocorax brasilianus

This small cormorant of the Texas coast can be hard to distinguish from the larger, but similar, Double-crested Cormorant. The Neotropic Cormorant is a different shape, with a longer tail and shorter beak. In the breeding season, it has a white border on the base of its beak and no tufts on its head.

SMALL

Phalacrocorax car

This cormorant is larger than the Double-crested Cormorant. It can be found along much of the Atlantic coast and sometimes shows up in the Great Lakes region. It has a white throat and, when seen in flight, white patches on the sides of its rump.

DANZENBAKER

Anhinga

Anhinga anhinga

This long-necked angler of the southeastern states can create quite a stir when it is found farther north than usual. The long pointed beak and very long neck help distinguish it from cormorants.

SMALL

Purple Gallinule

Porphyrio martinica

A brightly colored version of the Common Moorhen, the Purple Gallinule is usually found in the southeastern coastal states. It does wander, however, and has been found as far north as Newfoundland.

McCAW

What can I do
to help waterfowl?

By learning more about waterfowl, you have become even more connected to the natural world around you

WETLAND HABITATS are a very important part of our environment, and yet they are often regarded as "useless" because they are too wet for agriculture and they don't contain enough trees for forestry. Getting past this "how can we use it?" mentality is needed to ensure that a variety of habitats are left for wildlife. Supporting organizations such as the Nature Conservancy and Ducks Unlimited will help protect some of the wetland species that are featured in this book. For a more hands-on activity, you could help count ducks at a waterfowl staging area during migration or build and put up a nesting box. Species such as Wood Ducks, Hooded Mergansers, Common Mergansers, Common and Barrow's Goldeneyes, and Buffleheads will all use nest boxes. Other wildlife species, such as American Kestrels, Eastern Screech-Owls and Northern Flying Squirrels, may also use the boxes. Plans vary according to what species you want to attract, so figure out what may nest in your area and then contact a local naturalist club or the Wildlife Service, or surf the Net to find suitable nest box plans.

And don't forget that your interest alone is also very important. By learning more about waterfowl, you have become even more connected to the natural world around you. When you share your interest with others, the growing support for wildlife and their habitats increases.

A female Wood Duck in a nest box

DANZENBAKER

Cinnamon Teal • page 48

McCAW

American Black Duck • page 42

SMALL

Northern Pintail • page 52

SMALL

Blue-winged Teal • page 46

McCAW

Mallard • page 44

SMALL

Gadwall • page 36

SMALL

Green-winged Teal • page 54

SMALL

Northern Shoveler • page 50

SMALL

American Wigeon • page 40

	Slope of forehead	Beak size and color	Face pattern	Leg color	Other
Green-winged Teal	Steep	Small and gray, may have some yellowish edges	Light with a dark eyeline; usually no light spot at base of beak	Usually gray	May show a light line on upper part of undertail coverts
Blue-winged Teal	Gradual	Average and dark gray	Light with a dark eyeline; whitish spot at base of beak	Yellowish	Flanks more patterned than Cinnamon Teal
Cinnamon Teal	Gradual	Large and dark gray	Plainer overall than Blue-winged Teal	Yellowish	Flanks less patterned than Blue-winged Teal
Northern Shoveler	Gradual	Very large and orange with a darkish saddle	Dark and plain with an indistinct eyeline	Orange	
Mallard	Gradual	Average and orange with a dark saddle	Light with a dark eyeline	Orange	Body lighter and more patterned than American Black Duck
American Black Duck	Gradual	Average and dull green with a darkish saddle	Light with a dark eyeline	Orange	Body much darker and less patterned than Mallard
American Wigeon	Steep	Short and light gray with a dark tip	Light, often with a dark eye patch	Dark	Fairly plain flanks
Gadwall	Steep	Smaller than average and orange with a dark saddle	Light with an indistinct eyeline	Yellow	May show white speculum
Northern Pintail	Steepish	Smaller than average and gray	Plain and light	Gray	Long pointed tail and long slender neck

Canvasback/Redhead comparison

	Canvasback · pages 56, 57	Redhead · page 58, 59
Head and beak shape	Wedge-shaped	Steeper forehead
Head color	Male reddish brown	Male light reddish brown
Eye color	Male dark red	Male yellow
Beak color	Dark gray	Light gray with a dark tip
Back color	Male very light gray; female brownish gray	Male darker gray; female browner overall

Greater/Lesser Scaup comparison

Male — McCAW

Male — REAUME

Female — SMALL

Female — FAIRBAIRN

	Greater Scaup · page 64, 65	**Lesser Scaup** · page 66, 67
Head shape	Often squarish with a rounded or flat top; steep forehead	Often triangular with a peak on crown behind eye; less steep of a forehead
Male head color	Greenish, but could look purplish in some lights	Purplish, but may show some green
Beak	Large beak with a large black tip	Small beak with a small amount of black on tip
Wing stripe*	White stripe flows from secondaries into primaries (some Greaters may not have white in primaries)	Stripe is white in secondaries and gray in primaries (some Lessers may have white in primaries)
Overall size	Larger than Lesser, seen if two are side by side	Smaller than Greater, seen if two are side by side

*Seen in flight or when floating bird stretches and flaps.

King Eider female · page 69 — FLYNN

Common Eider female · page 73 — McCAW

King Eider first-year male · page 70 — FLYNN

Common Eider first-year male · page 73 — DANZENBAKER

King Eider male · page 68 — FLYNN

Common Eider male · page 72 — SMALL

	King Eider · page 68	Common Eider · page 72
Beak shape	Female has more rounded shape to feathered area at base of the beak; adult male's has large knob	Female has more pointed shape to feathered area at base of the beak; adult male's has no knob
Beak color	Female's is dark; first-year male's is orange; adult male's is multicolored	Female's is gray; first-year male's is grayish; adult male's is greenish or yellow
Back color	First-year male's is dark; adult male's is black	First-year male's has variable amounts of white; adult male's is white
Flank pattern	Female has crescents	Female has vertical barring

DANZENBAKER

Black male • page 82

FLYNN

Black female • page 82

McCAW

White-winged male • page 80

McCAW

White-winged first-spring female • page 80

SMALL

Surf male • page 78

SMALL

Surf female • page 79

	Surf Scoter · page 78	White-winged Scoter · page 80	Black Scoter · page 82
Adult male beak color	Orange with a black patch bordered by white	Orange with a black knob	Black with an orange knob
Beak shape	Large and deep, squarish at base	Long with lots of feathering that extends into the upper surface at the base. Adult males have a small knob.	More "regular duck"-shaped with a "normal" base. Adult males have a large orange knob.
Adult male head pattern	Black with white patches on forehead and nape	Black with white crescent under eye	All black
Female head pattern	Brown with variable whitish patches at base of beak, cheek and nape	Brown with variable whitish patches at base of beak and cheek	Dark brown cap with pale brown cheeks
Speculum	None	White	None

Goldeneyes comparison

Common male

Barrow's male

Common female

Barrow's female

McCAW

McCAW

SMALL

SMALL

	Common · page 90	Barrow's · page 92
Head shape	Almost triangular with a sloped forehead and slightly peaked crown	Blockish with a steep forehead, flat crown and often a bulge at nape
Male head color	Black, usually with a green iridescence	Black, usually with a purple iridescence
Beak shape	Deep at base	Shorter overall, making base look proportionally deeper
Female beak color	Black with varying amounts of yellow on tip, rarely all yellow	Mostly yellow with some black
White spot at base of male's beak	Circular	Crescent-shaped
Male scapulars	White with some thin black stripes	Black with some white spots

Female mergansers comparison

Common female • page 96

FLYNN

Red-breasted female • page 98

SMAL

Hooded female • page 94

SMAL

	Common Merganser	Red-breasted Merganser	Hooded Merganser
Head	Reddish brown with a short crest	Pale reddish brown with a longer but sparse crest	Dark brown with a long, thick, reddish brown crest
Beak	Long and orange with thick base going up part of the forehead	Thin, long and orange with no thick base	Thin, shorter and dark on top; yellowish on bottom
Throat	Distinct white patch	Indistinct pale area	Gray
Body length	Long	Long	Short

Winter loons comparison

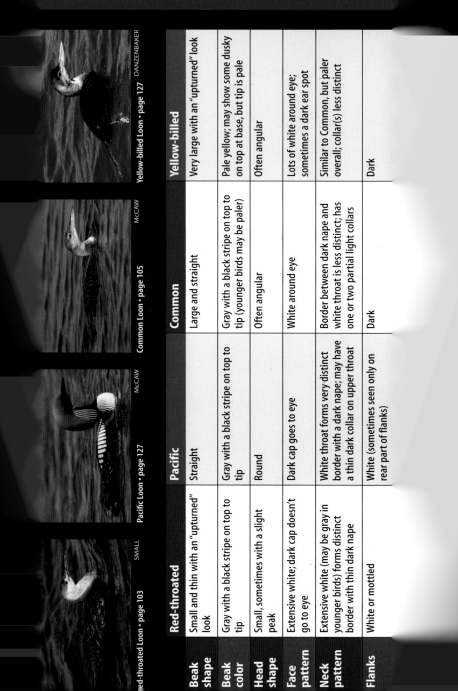

Red-throated Loon • page 103 (SMALL) — Pacific Loon • page 127 (McCAW) — Common Loon • page 105 (McCAW) — Yellow-billed Loon • page 127 (DANZENBAKER)

	Red-throated	Pacific	Common	Yellow-billed
Beak shape	Small and thin with an "upturned" look	Straight	Large and straight	Very large with an "upturned" look
Beak color	Gray with a black stripe on top to tip	Gray with a black stripe on top to tip	Gray with a black stripe on top to tip (younger birds may be paler)	Pale yellow; may show some dusky on top at base, but tip is pale
Head shape	Small, sometimes with a slight peak	Round	Often angular	Often angular
Face pattern	Extensive white; dark cap doesn't go to eye	Dark cap goes to eye	White around eye	Lots of white around eye; sometimes a dark ear spot
Neck pattern	Extensive white (may be gray in younger birds) forms distinct border with thin dark nape	White throat forms very distinct border with a dark nape; may have a thin dark collar on upper throat	Border between dark nape and white throat is less distinct; has one or two partial light collars	Similar to Common, but paler overall; collar(s) less distinct
Flanks	White or mottled	White (sometimes seen only on rear part of flanks)	Dark	Dark

Winter grebes comparison

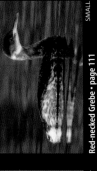

Pied-billed Grebe · page 107 SMALL

Eared Grebe · page 113 SMALL

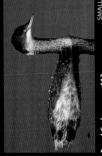

Horned Grebe · page 109 SMALL

Red-necked Grebe · page 111 SMALL

	Pied-billed	Eared	Horned	Red-necked
Beak shape	Thick, almost blunt	Very thin, upturned, pointed	Thin and straight	Long, strong-looking, pointed
Beak color	Light gray or buffy; may show partial ring	Gray	Gray with a light tip	Yellowish
Neck color	Buffy or reddish	Mostly dark or dusky	Mostly white with black on the back of neck	Gray or reddish
Head markings	Brownish head with thin white eyering and whitish throat	Dark head with white throat and white behind dark cheeks	Dark cap with white cheeks and dark nape	Dusky head, darker on cap, with light patch behind cheeks

Flight comparison

Geese & Swans

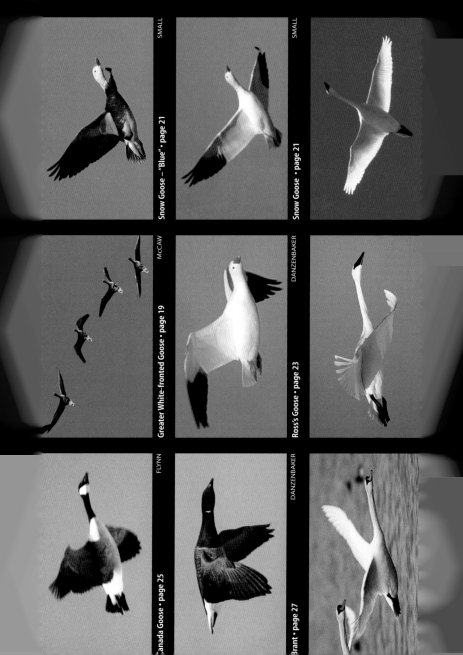

SMALL

Snow Goose — "Blue" • page 21

SMALL

Snow Goose • page 21

McCAW

Greater White-fronted Goose • page 19

DANZENBAKER

Ross's Goose • page 23

FLYNN

Canada Goose • page 25

DANZENBAKER

Brant • page 27

DANZENBAKER

American Wigeon male · page 41

DANZENBAKER

Green-winged Teal · page 55

DANZENBAKER

Gadwall male · page 37

McCAW

Mallard male · page 45

DANZENBAKER

Northern Pintail male · page 53

DANZENBAKER

American Black Duck male · page 43

DANZENBAKER

Divers

MCCAW

Ring-necked Duck male · page 61

DANZENBAKER

Tufted Duck male · page 63

DANZENBAKER

FLYNN

Redhead female · page 59

SMALL

Lesser Scaup male · page 67

DANZENBAKER

FLYNN

Redhead male · page 59

MCCAW

edhead male · page 64

DANZENBAKER

SMALL

White-winged Scoter male • page 81

FAIRBAIRN

Bufflehead male • page 89

DANZENBAKER

DANZENBAKER

Surf Scoter male • page 79

SMALL

Bufflehead female • page 89

DANZENBAKER

Hooded Merganser male • page 97

DANZENBAKER

Black Scoter male • page 83

DANZENBAKER

Red-breasted Merganser female • page 98

DANZENBAKER

Female divers comparison

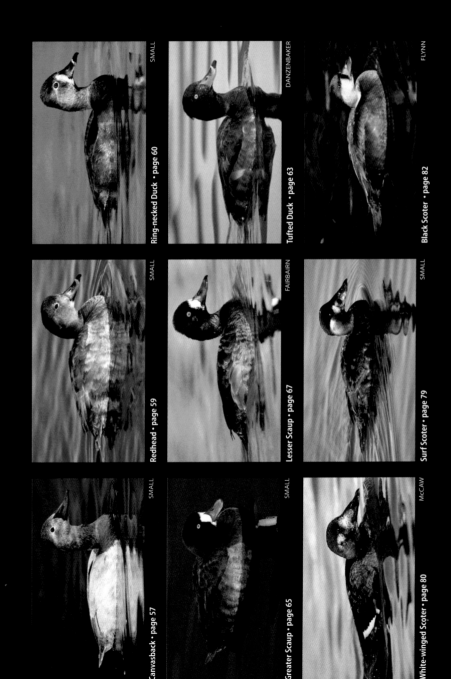

SMALL

Ring-necked Duck • page 60

DANZENBAKER

Tufted Duck • page 63

FLYNN

Black Scoter • page 82

SMALL

Redhead • page 59

FAIRBAIRN

Lesser Scaup • page 67

SMALL

Surf Scoter • page 79

SMALL

Canvasback • page 57

SMALL

Greater Scaup • page 65

McCAW

White-winged Scoter • page 80

McCAW

Common Goldeye · page 90

SMALL

Barrow's Goldeneye · page 92

Hooded Merganser · page 94

FAIRBAIRN

Bufflehead · page 88

FAIRBAIRN

Long-tailed Duck – winter · page 85

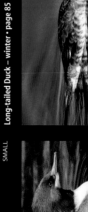

Red-breasted Merganser · page 98

SMALL

Harlequin Duck · page 77

SMALL

Ruddy Duck · page 101

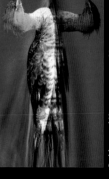
FLYNN

Common Merganser · page 96

Male ducks comparison

Northern Pintail • page 52

SMALL

Gadwall • page 36

SMAL

American Black Duck • page 42

FLYNN

Black/Mallard Cross • page 42

McCAW

Red-breasted Marganser • page 98

McCAW

Mallard • page 44

McCAW

Common Merganser • page 96

Shoveler • page 50

SMALL

King Eider • page 68   FLYNN

Common Eider • page 72   FLYNN

American Wigeon • page 40   SMALL

Eurasian Wigeon • page 38   SMALL

Green-winged Teal • page 54   FAIRBAIRN

Wood Duck • page 34   McCAW

Blue-winged Teal • page 46   McCAW

Cinnamon Teal • page 48   SMALL

Male ducks comparison

Tufted Duck • page 62 — McCAW

Ring-necked Duck • page 60 — McCAW

Greater Scaup • page 64 — FAIRBAIRN

Lesser Scaup • page 66 — McCAW

Common Goldeneye • page 90 — McCAW

Bufflehead • page 88 — McCAW

Barrow's Goldeneye • page 92 — SMALL

Hooded Merganser • page 94 — FAIRBAIRN

Canvasback • page 56   SMALL

Surf Scoter • page 78   SMALL

Redhead • page 58   SMALL

Black Scoter • page 82   DANZENBAKER

Harlequin Duck • page 76   McCAW

White-winged Scoter • page 80   McCAW

Long-tailed Duck (winter) • page 84   FLYNN

Ruddy Duck • page 100   McCAW

References

THERE ARE MANY references on waterfowl, especially ducks, for readers who wish to delve further into these birds' lives. *The Birds of North America*, edited by Poole and Gill, includes heaps of information on waterfowl as collected by the scientific community.

Annotated Checklist of the Birds of Ontario (second edition). R.D. James, 1991. Royal Ontario Museum.

Atlas of the Breeding Birds of Ontario. M.D. Cadman, P.F.J. Eagles and F.M. Helleiner, 1987. University of Waterloo Press.

The Audubon Society Encyclopedia of North American Birds. John K. Terres, 1991. Wings Books.

The Birder's Handbook. P.R. Ehrlich, D.S. Dobkin and D. Wheye, 1988. Fireside/Simon and Schuster.

Birds and Trees of North America. Rex Brasher. 1962. Rowman and Littlefield.

The Birds of Canada (revised edition). W. Earl Godfrey, 1986. National Museums of Canada.

The Birds of North America. Series published by the Academy of Natural Sciences of Philadelphia and the American Ornithologists' Union.

Birds of North America. K. Kaufman, 2000. Houghton Mifflin.

Birds of the West Coast, Volume 2. J.F. Lansdowne, 1980. M.F. Feheley Arts Company Ltd.

Check-list of North American Birds, 1998. The American Ornithologists' Union.

The Dictionary of American Bird Names (revised edition). E.A. Choate, 1985. Harvard Common Press.

The Distinctive Harlequin. J. Wilburn. *Bird Watcher's Digest*, March/April 1986.

Ducks, Geese and Swans of North America. Frank C. Bellrose, 1976. Stackpole Books.

Ducks of Canada and the Northern Hemisphere. J. Gooders and T. Boyer, 1986. Dragon's World Limited.

Ducks in the Wild: Conserving Waterfowl and Their Habitats. P.A. Johnsgard, 1992. Prentice Hall General Reference.

Field Guide to the Birds of North America. National Geographic Society, 1987.

The Firefly Encyclopedia of Birds. C. Perrins, 2003. Firefly Books.

Food Piracy by American Wigeons on American Coots. R.A. Knapton and B. Knudsen, 1978. *Canadian Field-Naturalist* 92(4): 403–404.

A Guide to Field Identification: Birds of North America. C.S. Robbins, B. Bruun and H.S. Zim, 1966. Golden Press.

John James Audubon: Writings and Drawings. Edited by C. Irmscher, 1999. The Library of America.

Life Histories of North American Wild Fowl, Parts 1 and 2. Edited by A.C. Bent, 1923 and 1925. U.S. National Museum.

National Audubon Society Field Guide to North American Birds – Eastern Region. J. Bull and J. Farrand, Jr., 1994. Alfred A. Knopf.

North American Game Birds. M. Hehner, C. Dorsey and Greg Breining, 1996. Cy DeCosse Incorporated.

North American Geese. R. Alison. *Wild Bird*, April 1992.

Peterson Field Guides: Advance Birding. Kenn Kaufman, 1990. Houghton Mifflin.

Peterson Field Guides: Eastern Birds. R.T. Peterson. Houghton Mifflin.

Peterson Natural History Companions: Lives of North American Birds. Kenn Kaufman, 1996. Houghton Mifflin.

The Practiced Eye: Female Dabbling Ducks. Kenn Kaufman. American Birds, Winter 1988.

Seasonal Status of Birds: Point Pelee National Park and Vicinity. Compiled by J.R. Graham, 1996.

The Sibley Guide to Birdlife and Behaviour. D.A. Sibley, 2001. Alfred A. Knopf.

The Sibley Guide to Birds. D.A. Sibley, 2000. Alfred A. Knopf.

Stokes Field Guide to Birds: Eastern Region. D. and L. Stokes, 1996. Little, Brown.

Studer's Popular Ornithology: The Birds of North America. Edited by J.H. Studer, 1881. Harrison House.

Thoreau on Birds. Henry David Thoreau, 1910. Beacon Press.

Waterfowl: An Identification Guide. S. Madge and H. Burn, 1988. Houghton Mifflin.

Waterfowl: Their Biology and Natural History. P.A. Johnsgard, 1968. University of Nebraska Press.

Author's notes

To Mom and Dad,

When all the other parents had to drive their kids to baseball practice, mine had to drive me to the local sewage lagoons so I could watch the ducks instead. Thanks!

SPECIAL THANKS to Ron Lohr and Richard Tofflemire for reviewing earlier drafts. This book would not have been possible without the talent, generosity and patience of the photographers.

Credits

Photography: Mike Danzenbaker, Scott Fairbairn, Jim Flynn, Jean Iron, Robert McCaw, John Reaume, Brian E. Small

The range maps throughout this book were generously provided by WILDSPACE™ 2002; WILDSPACE™ – digital hemispheric range maps for the breeding birds of Canada. Canadian Wildlife Service, Ontario Region, Ottawa, Ontario.

Index

By the same author

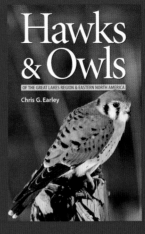

"An excellent identification guide... the photos are well chosen... the text is clear and concise."
— *Minneapolis Star Tribune*

"Excellent... Earley's concise volume is well constructed and worth adding to any falconer or birder's library."
— *Hawk Chalk*

"Well-done, birder-friendly guides that fit easily into any field pack."
— *BirdWatcher's Digest*

"Makes identifying these remarkable and diverse families of birds as easy as possible." —*Princeton Times of Trenton*

"The most comprehensive information on several targeted species, packed in a colorful, convenient format."
— *Bird Times*

"Excellent information, more than 200 quality color photographs and delightful prose make these must-have guides."
— *Montreal Gazette*